Cohesive Writing

Why Concept Is Not Enough

Carol Jago

HEINEMANN
Portsmouth, NH

Heinemann

A division of Reed Elsevier Inc.

361 Hanover Street

Portsmouth, NH 03801–3912

www.heinemann.com

Offices and agents throughout the world

The author and publisher wish to thank those who have generously given permission to reprint borrowed materials:

Excerpts in Chapter Two from "Be Careful What You Ask For" by Craig Cotich and Joan Cotich are reprinted from *California English*, June 2001: Volume 6, No. 5. Published by the California Association of Teachers of English. Reprinted with permission.

The "Grammar Crime Hot Sheet" in Chapter Five is reprinted from "Grammar Crimes? Do the Time!" by Carole LeCren in *California English*, Spring 1998: Volume 3, No. 3. Published by the California Association of Teachers of English. Reprinted with permission.

Passages on responding to student writing in Chapter Five are reprinted from *Voices in the Middle*, September 2001. Copyright © 2001 by the National Council of Teachers of English. Reprinted with permission.

Library of Congress Cataloging-in-Publication Data

Jago, Carol, 1951–

    Cohesive writing : why concept is not enough / Carol Jago.

      p. cm.

    Includes bibliographical references and index.

    ISBN 0-86709-531-8

      1. English language—Composition and exercises—Study and teaching (Secondary)—United States. 2. Language arts (Secondary)—United States. I. Title.

LB1631 .J36 2002

808'.042'071273—dc21   2001043876

Editor: Lisa Luedeke

Production editor: Elizabeth Valway

Typesetter: House of Equations, Inc.

Cover design: Cathy Hawkes, Cat and Mouse

Cover photo: Dana White

Manufacturing: Steve Bernier

Printed in the United States of America on acid-free paper

06 05 04 03 02 RRD 1 2 3 4 5

What is written without effort is in general read without pleasure.
—*Samuel Johnson*

A writer is a person who enters into sustained relations with the language for experiment and experience not available in any other way.
—*William Stafford*

Contents

List of Figures   vii

Foreword   ix

Acknowledgments   xi

Introduction   1

1   Cohesive Writing—The Method   7
     Getting Started   8
     Question Papers   9
     Moving from Freewriting to Drafting   13
     Prompts That Stimulate Thoughtful Response   14

2   Teaching Informational and Persuasive Writing   23
     Reading Like a Writer   24
     Deconstructing What Professional Essayists Do   27
     Writing to Persuade   30

3   Teaching Narrative Writing   39
     The Good, the Bad, and the Worrisome   48
     Narrative Standards   49
     Teaching Narration Piecemeal   50
     Autobiographical Narration—The Dread College Essay   54

Contents

4   Writing About Literature   61
    Assessment Instruments and Rubrics   61
    Student Papers and Scoring Guides   62
    Multiple Traits Scoring   66
    One English Department's Rubric   67
    Scaffolding for Struggling Writers   74
    Five Things to Do with a Quotation   77
    Culminating Assignments That Don't Feel Like Hard Work   80

5   Cohesive Writing—The Product   83
    The Writing Process Revisited   83
    Learning to Write by Writing   85
    A Five-Day Writing Plan   88
    When "Awk" Isn't Enough   95
    Addressing Mechanical Errors   97
    Peer Response   98
    Authentic Revision   104
    Self-Assessment   107

6   Cohesive Writing Matters   117

Bibliography   121

About the Author   123

Index   124

List of Figures

2–1   Analyzing a Published Essay   26
2–2   Informational and Persuasive Writing Compared   32
4–1   California Standards Test Scoring Rubric: 63
       Grade 7 Writing Task
4–2   Santa Monica High School English Department   68
       Analytical Essay Scoring Guide, Grades 9–12
4–3   Reflection Chart   75
5–1   A Five-Day Writing Plan   89
5–2   Point and Block Methods Compared   90
5–3   Grammar Crime Hot Sheet   100
5–4   Peer Response Sheet   102
5–5   Writers Need Readers   104
5–6   Letters Home   105
5–7   Evaluating Your Revision   108
5–8   Portfolio Checklist   112
5–9   Reading Log   113
5–10   Portfolio Self-Assessment   114

Foreword

This is supposed to be a foreword for a book on teaching writing. As such, it should probably offer observations about the composing process, critical comments about the ideas Carol puts forth in this book. It could, I suppose, explain how I, a university teacher in Houston, Texas, with a specialty in secondary reading, am connected with Carol, a high school teacher in Santa Monica, California, with a specialty in secondary writing. It should do all those things, all those things and more. It won't. Instead, this foreword offers a heartfelt thank-you to Carol for writing with clarity and passion, for raising the standard on how to help students meet standards, for offering this reader a moment of cohesion at a time when much is falling apart.

Today is September 19, 2001. It is a mere eight days after the destruction of the World Trade Center, the destruction at the Pentagon, the destruction of a field in Pennsylvania. It is a mere eight days after thousands of lives were lost; thousands more forever changed.

And at this moment, I'm on a plane, Continental flight 3823, flying far too far from my home to go off to work with teachers. My briefcase is in the seat across the aisle from me. The tray table on the seatback of the seat next to me is down, holding Carol's manuscript, a cup of coffee, my watch, a pen. My tray table is down, holding my laptop computer. My seat is reclined, for there is no chance of crowding anyone behind me. A blanket warms my lap; another is draped over the seat in front in case I should want it. Pillows—seven of them—are stacked in the seat diagonally across the aisle from me. No children crying. No quiet snoring of tired businessmen. Only eight others on this plane. I'm lonely and want to be home with my children, my husband, my friends.

Work, I decided early into the flight. I pulled out the manuscript of this book suspecting I'd manage at best a few chapters, my recent attention span. Instead, two hours later, I realized that for the first time since last Tuesday I had read a book—no, been lost in a book. For two hours, I sat in a classroom peering over the shoulder of a skilled teacher, reading her students' papers and analyzing transcripts of class discussions and teacher-student conferences, learning how to evaluate student writing, discovering how to help students write cohesively—to create writing that holds together. I scribbled note after note in the margins: "Yes! I can do that" or "Must try this with my students" and "Do this next week with Monday's class" and the wish "Why didn't I think of that?" For two hours and 133 pages I was under the spell of a mentor who step at a time taught her students to write critically, persuasively, descriptively—write powerfully—while page at a time tutored this reader in writing, in teaching, in understanding how to be far more than standard in a time governed by standards. Grounded in theory but soaring with practical lessons, *Cohesive Writing* offered me guidance in writing instruction like I've never read before.

For two hours, I wasn't alone on a near-empty plane traveling far from my home and those of my heart. I was in Carol's classroom, with her kids and her teaching, her wit and her wisdom. My thanks to Carol for that.

Kylene Beers
Editor, *Voices from the Middle*
University of Houston

Acknowledgments

To Michael, who would have rather been gardening than editing, and to my students, who have learned that cultivating their garden helps makes this the best of all possible worlds. *Cela est bien dit, répondit Candide, mais il faut cultiver notre jardin.*

Introduction

Once upon a time James Britton, Donald Graves, Peter Elbow, Dixie Gotswami, and James Gray—giants on the earth—showed us new ways to think about writing. Their work, and the work of others who followed their lead, brought about tremendous changes in curriculum and instruction. I can't imagine an English teacher in this country, novice or expert, who isn't familiar with writing as a process thanks to them. So influential has been their work that the English Language Arts standards documents of many states invariably include references to the essential elements of the writing process. According to a report by the GED Testing Service, *Alignment of National and State Standards* (Woodward 1999):

> Although the terminology related to the writing process—often referred to as process writing—may vary slightly among states, the overall perception of how the process functions remains steadfast. States regard prewriting, drafting, revision, editing, and publishing as the essential features of the process and stress that the process itself is recursive. (83)

The work of these innovators has received such widespread acceptance that most current assessment instruments—NAEP (National Assessment of Educational Progress), statewide language arts tests, as well as high school exit exams and GEDs—include a direct writing sample.

In many ways this is a dream come true for advocates of process writing. Yet we must be careful what we wish for.

We accept that assessment drives instruction. For this reason most English teachers cheered the appearance of writing prompts on standardized tests. We were delighted that students would be required to do more than identify run-on sentences, misspellings, and misplaced modifiers. Requiring students to produce a page or two of well-written prose on state tests seemed to validate our writing programs and send a powerful message to students that "writing matters." Writing across the curriculum became more and more the norm in middle and high school classrooms. Writing had truly become a priority. What blindsided us was the way results of state and national assessments would be used to demonstrate what a dreadful job teachers were doing.

NAEP, which is considered the nation's report card, describes student results in writing with three achievement levels: basic, proficient, and advanced. On the 1998 NAEP Writing Assessment, only 27 percent of students nationwide in eighth grade and 22 percent of those in the twelfth grade performed at the proficient level. One percent of students performed at the advanced level. These results sound pretty grim until one examines the criteria for proficiency. Students performing at the proficient level in the eighth grade are expected to be able to:

- create an effective response to the task in form, content, and language;
- demonstrate an awareness of the intended audience;
- use effective organization appropriate to the task;
- use sufficient elaboration to clarify and enhance the central idea;
- use language appropriate to the task and intended audience; and
- have few errors in spelling, grammar, punctuation, and capitalization that interfere with communication.
  http://nces.ed.gov/nationsreportcard/writing/achieveall.asp#grade8

At the twelfth-grade level students' responses must demonstrate "convincing" elaboration and use "logical and observable organization."

Don't misunderstand me; we *should* set high standards for student writing. Writing matters a great deal both in college and in the workplace, and students who write well have a tremendous advantage. Teachers should be working toward helping every student to become what NAEP describes as proficient. Unfortunately most newspapers report only the bad news. Headlines proclaim, "Three out of four students *fail!*" then themselves fail to describe what the scores represent in terms of student achievement. In a regular—not an honors—class I have rarely seen more than one in four students able to write at the level NAEP deems proficient. Not that we aren't working toward it, but most fifteen-year-olds simply aren't there yet. Few reporters seem interested in a story about how Hilda is learning to vary her sentence structure or how Robby has curbed his use of the ubiquitous adverb "really." No headlines here.

On April 8, 2000, Colorado's Lieutenant Governor Joe Rogers did garner headlines with his Uncensored Conference on Youth Education. What was unique about this summit was that, instead of gathering the usual suspects, Rogers invited 1,300 high school students to the University of Denver to hear their suggestions for improving the quality of education. In the area of writing, organizers posed two simple questions:

- Why are students having problems with writing?
- How can we do a better job of teaching students to write well?

These Colorado teenagers defined the problem:

- Teachers are not adequately teaching students to write.
- The subject matter is not interesting. Students insisted that what they wrote about was strongly connected to how well they wrote about a subject.
- Early education is inadequate.
- Students have weak basic skills. Students said they received initial instruction in grammar, writing, and spelling, but the skills were not enforced consistently.

- Reading skills are low.
- Too much emphasis on structure and too many rules are hindering students' ability to write creatively. At the same time students felt that the structure of language such as syntax and grammar is not taught consistently or explained well.
- Vocabulary skills are weak.
- Language skills are weak, especially for students acquiring English as a second langugage.
- Expectations for student performance are unclear and vary widely among teachers.
- Spelling skills are poor.

Even more interesting than students' clear definition of the problem were their top ten solutions:

- Encourage teachers to be more responsive to students. Students need more individual attention and more practical support.
- Give more flexibility and freedom in choosing subject matter for writing.
- Provide early education in reading, writing, and grammar. (Teachers know these things are taught in the early grades. Perhaps what these students are telling us is, "Help us realize that these skills are important—that we will need them later on!")
- Teach basics.
- Allow more creativity. Students want more opportunities for creative writing and the freedom to develop their own writing style.
- Provide more writing practice.
- Establish and enforce standards.
- Teach grammar skills.
- Develop reading skills.
- Gear the pace and content according to each student's writing level, and be more supportive of individual learning.

This report is powerful in that it refutes the notion that teenagers don't value education. These Colorado kids care that they haven't been adequately prepared to write well and believe that teachers could be doing a better job. The complete report, which includes student views on reading, mathematics, discipline, and dropout rates, can be found at *<www.coloradouncensored.org>*. Out of the mouths of babes . . .

I teach at a large public high school of 3,200, and the students I work with would by and large agree with their Colorado counterparts. Santa Monica High School's demographic profile almost exactly matches that of California both in terms of socioeconomics and ethnicity. We have no "majority" population. Over forty-five languages are spoken. Children of movie stars sit next to homeless kids, teenage mothers next to National Merit Scholars. On nationally normed tests we come in at about the 55th percentile, a comfortable score for any large, diverse school. But ranking is deceptive. Like California, Santa Monica High School is stubbornly bipolar. We have a large percentage of high-performing students whose scores mask the number of children who fall far below that 55th percentile. These numbers are the more uncomfortable to live with as the high-performing students are for the most part white and Asian and from the more affluent side of town while the greatest number of our low-performing students are Latino and African American.

I wish I were able to trumpet solutions and unveil a blueprint for eliminating any such troubling achievement gap. Despite grappling with this issue for over fifteen years, our committed, caring, students, parents, teachers, counselors, and administrators are still experimenting with programs and methods aimed at engaging all students in a rigorous curriculum. We have found no magic bullet. What you will find in this book is evidence of successful practices, classroom strategies for teaching writing that have resulted in significant growth for many of my students.

My approach has deeply influenced by the thinking of Britton, Graves, Gray, and the others, and by the writing of the remarkable students I have taught over the past twenty-five years. It has also been influenced by the current political climate in education. California and many other states require students to pass exit exams. Students who are not able to develop an essay in an organized fashion with few mechanical errors will no longer receive a high school diploma. It is a teacher's professional responsibility to prepare students for these high-stakes tests. I also believe it is essential to show teenagers how writing can be a way to learn about themselves, a tool for sorting out the complex inner landscape. Though these two agendas may sometimes compete for classroom time, they are not mutually exclusive.

I have a few ideas about how teachers can do both. Let me show you.

ONE

Cohesive Writing—The Method

When we describe something as "cohesive" we mean that the thing holds together, that separate pieces stick or cling firmly to one another to create the whole. In the physical world cohesion is the force that holds molecules together. The architect Frank Lloyd Wright drew up cohesive building plans, balancing form and function to create livable houses that were also works of art. The artful hostess brings together people likely to interest one another around a bountiful table in order to create a cohesive dinner party. The gardener places shrubs and flowers with attention to height, color, and seasonal glory, carefully considering how each element adds to the cohesiveness of the whole. So it is with cohesive writing. Writers wrestle with ideas, balance form and function, push words this way and that, take care with syntax and diction, and employ imagery and metaphor until a cohesive message emerges.

Though full of promise, student writing typically lacks cohesion. As a result, their messages are garbled. Parts of student essays may sparkle, but the whole is seldom "harmoniously accordant" (*The Oxford English Dictionary*'s definition for *coherent*). Discord and cacophony better describe many of my students' initial products. The fault is not in the stars or in the students but in ourselves. Our methods of teaching writing lack cohesion. Within the same English Department, one teacher's writing program may consist entirely of personal journals while down the hall another assigns five-paragraph essays. No wonder students are confused. On the pages that follow, I present an effective approach for helping students write cohesively and produce written work in which the different aspects of their writing hold together fast. It is not a lockstep lesson plan or simple recipe. It is an organized, coherent method that works.

Getting Started

In her book, *Bird by Bird: Some Instructions on Writing and Life* (1994), Anne Lamott tells a story about her brother, ten at the time, who was working on a bird report that he had had three months to write. It was due the next morning. (This story will sound familiar to any parent of a ten-year-old boy.) Sitting at the kitchen table, surrounded by paper and pencils and a pile of books on birds, he was paralyzed by the hugeness of the task and close to tears. Anne's father sat down beside him, put an arm around his shoulder and said, "Bird by bird, buddy. Just take it bird by bird."

I know no better advice for young writers. Most of my students who don't complete their work for class are afflicted with the same paralysis. It is not that they can't do the assignment. It is not that they don't want to do the assignment. They just can't figure out where to begin. Inertia, rather than indolence, keeps those pages blank.

When I ask such students why their papers are late, they often shrug and assure me they are working on them. This is not a lie. They are. They just can't bring themselves to make the first mark on the page. I believe that these students who appear to be the class "flakes," may in fact be the class perfectionists, unwilling to write a single word until they are sure it's the best word.

In *Bird by Bird*, Anne Lamott lays out a series of lessons to help writers mired in the slough of perfectionism. She recommends starting small. Instead of beginning with an outline for a due-tomorrow term paper or a cast of characters for the Great American Novel, she advises students to write as much as they can see through a one-inch picture frame. One paragraph. One point. One bird.

E. L. Doctorow, National Book Award–winning author of *Ragtime*, said, "writing a novel is like driving a car at night. You can see only as far as your headlights, but you can make the whole trip this way."

For students paralyzed by the thought of a 1,000-word essay, such advice is liberating. Don't worry about all 1,000 words. Write the first 50, and the remaining 950 will follow. You can always revise them later.

Physicists use the term *inertia* to describe the property of matter in which it continues in its existing state, whether at rest or in motion, unless altered by an external force. I often have students use an inertia exercise, having them write nonstop for fifteen minutes. If they run out of things to say, I tell them to recopy the last word over and over until a new one comes to mind. I remind students that such free-form writing is not what I expect to see on their finished papers, but that what we have done is exerted an external force on their static inertia. Once their words begin flowing, inertia of motion takes over.

Question Papers

Another method that helps students get started when writing about a piece of literature is a question paper. I am fairly certain that Claire Pelton was the originator of this lesson, but as with so many good teaching ideas, over the years it has gone through the sausage-maker in my brain and emerged in a somewhat different form.

Writing responses to literature, while not one of the three NAEP writing types (narrative, informative, and persuasive), commonly appears as part of state and district writing assessments. In California, students are asked to write a response to literature both at the seventh-grade level and as part of an exit exam. This is also one of the most common writing assignments in high school. Given that the content of most English classes is literature, it makes sense that teachers would assign such papers. For many students, such writing seems very removed from their lives—school for school's sake at its worst; consequently, such essays are often the worst that students write all semester. Parroting what the teacher told them about *Romeo and Juliet* or *Lord of the Flies*, students patch together unrelated points, cobble together a few quotes, and type the whole thing up hoping it will pass muster.

You can make writing about literature more authentic by having students begin with their own questions. The Question Paper assignment encourages students to generate questions about the poem or story they plan to analyze and then to posit possible, tentative answers to their own questions. The task is much easier to model for students than to explain so I offer them the following question paper based upon Lord Byron's "She Walks in Beauty." I purposely choose this text because students find it appealing yet relatively opaque. I want to show them how questioning the text can help a writer figure out what needs to be said about the poem.

She Walks in Beauty

I

She walks in beauty, like the night,
    Of cloudless climes and starry skies;
And all that's best of dark and bright
    Meet in her aspect and her eyes:
Thus mellowed to that tender light
    Which heaven to gaudy day denies.

II

One shade the more, one ray the less,
    Had half impaired the nameless grace
Which waves in every raven tress,
    Or softly lightens o'er her face;
Where thoughts serenely sweet express
    How pure, how dear their dwelling place.

III

And on that cheek, and o'er that brow,
    So soft, so calm, yet so eloquent,
The smiles that win, the tints that glow,
    But tell of days in goodness spent,
A mind at peace with all below,
    A heart whose love is innocent!

Model Question Paper on "She Walks in Beauty"

I really like the sound of the first line about walking in beauty "like the night," but I'm not really sure why beauty should be anything like the night at all. OK, Byron says there are starry skies and so I guess the stars shine in her eyes but couldn't he also be saying that the girl looks better in the dark? I mean maybe the night covers up her blemishes or something. I guess not because he has a really gentle line to describe this, "mellowed to that tender night." I wonder if what he means by comparing this to "gaudy day" is like seeing someone in really harsh fluorescent light. What is he talking about in the second stanza though? I don't get what this "one shade the more and one ray the less" means except that he likes her black hair a lot. Maybe he's saying that the look on her face is so sweet because her thoughts are so happy to be inside a beautiful head. I don't know. Maybe not. Maybe the poet is saying that she is such a fundamentally good person, inside and out, mind and heart, that she cannot help but "walk in beauty."

Together we read the poem and the model question paper. I then ask students how writing this paper seemed to help the student understand the poem. My students always see how questioning the text allowed the reader to explore the piece of literature without worrying about being right or wrong. I make sure they notice how the writer revises early interpretations, pushing himself to understand more clearly what the poem is saying. A question paper is a kind of dialogue between the writer and himself.

We make a list on the board of the kinds of questions and sentence openers that encourage thoughtfulness and stimulate unexpected answers:

- I wonder . . .
- How?
- Why?
- Maybe . . .
- It's possible that . . .

Students then break up into small groups, each with a different poem as the impetus for a question paper. Sometimes we use six different poems by the same author. Other times I choose six poems on a similar theme or subject. Students read the poem aloud, write for fifteen minutes nonstop (I let them go for twenty if the class seems really engaged in their writing), and then share what they have written in their groups. I encourage them to let the read-around lead to conversation about the poem. This isn't a case where we are looking for the "best" paper but rather an exercise in letting one idea fuel another.

At the end of class, I bring everyone together for a metacognitive dialogue. It is not enough that students should walk away saying "Whew, that wasn't too bad." I want them to understand *why* we did what we did. If they haven't internalized the idea that writing a question paper can help them write more thoughtfully about literature, I have merely kept them busy for an hour. What I'm trying to teach them about writing is much bigger than this. I hope they gain an approach for getting started on a paper. Usually they do.

Ms. Jago: So what happened when you started writing with your own questions?

Ryan: It was good. Easy. I've always got questions. It's the answers that I'm not so good at.

Anoushka: But I was in your group, Ryan, and you ended up answering all your questions. What I can't understand is how we answered questions that what we didn't know we knew the answers to.

Ryan: Yeah. And the hard questions were the best ones to try to answer. We had Adrienne Rich's "Aunt Jennifer's Tigers," and I was clueless at first about the tigers being creatures in the rug or whatever but as soon as I wrote, "What does wool and needles have to do with tigers?" I got it. It's weird.

Brent: Well, we had a really hard poem, Margaret Atwood's "This Is a Photograph of Me" and I just wrote a whole list of questions before I tried to answer any of them. But the questions changed. I think you tricked us, Mrs. Jago.

Ms. Jago: What do you mean, "Tricked you"?

Brent: You know, like getting us to keep going back to the poem for another question. Every time I went back I had to reread a line or two. Very tricky.

Anoushka: I did that too!

Ms. Jago: And maybe your questions "changed" as you say, Brent, because you saw more in the line the second time around. Do you think this was a good way of getting started? If I asked you to write a short essay on this poem tonight [*huge groans*]—wait, I'm not asking you to do this, only to consider the idea. If I assigned an essay on this poem, do you think you would have a place to begin?

Ryan: This would be better than if you just handed us the poems with one of your hard questions. But I'm glad we don't have to write an essay tonight.

Moving from Freewriting to Drafting

Students often confuse such "freewriting" exercises with a first draft. My students like writing question papers so much that they periodically ask if they can write one instead of an essay. I say "yes and no." Yes, they can use a question paper to discover what it is they have to say about the book and generate a thesis. No, the essay must appear in traditional form, developing from thesis through analysis and evidence to conclusion. It is important to help students distinguish between writing that helps them explore what it is that they have to say and a first attempt at an essay. In many ways a "quickwrite" and question papers are antithetical to the conventional expository essay. Instead of arguing a position, the writer takes up many, sometimes conflicting, positions. I believe that this kind of informal writing helps students to generate much richer and more cohesive products.

In this student sample, the writer explores her questions about Amy Tan's *The Joy Luck Club* and suggests an interesting idea for a thesis for her essay.

Question Paper on *The Joy Luck Club*

All through this book I have still been wondering about that daughter's mother in the first chapter. Before she died, she told her daughter about two children she had in China but was forced to leave them in the middle of the road because times were getting unbearable. I wonder what ever happened to these children who must be June's sisters or brothers. Does June often wonder about them? Did the mother ever wonder about the fate of her two forgotten children? Are they even alive? I know that if I had two siblings somewhere I would do anything in my power to find them because I would have so much curiosity.

Maybe the reason the mother never tried to find them is because those memories are very painful to her and she feels guilty for abandoning two children, then going to a new land to have more. She probably felt that at least her daughter has a right to know about them but she (the mother) made it clear that she didn't want to find them and would never help her to find them. Maybe it is this untold story that creates the tension between mother and daughter that plays out in all kinds of ways in the book.

—Marni Kamins, tenth grade

I don't know that Marni would have discovered such an intriguing idea had she been worried about syntax, diction, evidence, and organization. Inviting her to write freely about the book before sitting down to a first draft, helped her find a thesis that interested her. Suddenly writing about literature was less artificial, more authentic.

Prompts That Stimulate Thoughtful Response

Such a self-constructed response to literature is not the only kind of writing middle and high school teachers should be assigning. In order to prepare students for various writing assessments as well as real-world writing tasks, students must also be taught how to respond to a set prompt.

Many of my reluctant scholars prefer that I should be the one to set the question. I have also found that, left on their own, students seem to revert to a book-report type of response instead of analysis— as in this opening paragraph of a finished essay on Sylvia Plath's *The Bell Jar* by a struggling tenth-grade student, Alicia Escalera.

The Bell Jar by Sylvia Plath is an interesting novel. It is interesting in the way it is presented and the unique characters. The main char-

acter, Esther goes crazy and brings the reader in as if they are there.
The reader learns a new perspective on certain subjects such as children, marrige (sic), etc.

This student would, I believe, have benefited from a prompt that di-
rected her thinking toward analysis. Alicia has ideas about the novel,
but without a prompt to direct her, she is currently only able describe
what happens and then how these events affect her. Rather than prob-
ing the causes of the main character's behavior, she wrote, "I began to
feel sorry for her, and it felt as if I was a friend of hers." The final sentence of this essay convinced me that this student had had powerful
personal response to Sylvia Plath, yet what she wrote was almost
incoherent:

> To just stop and look at things, ideas and even if you don't like them,
> or they scare you, stop and explore them you will be a knowledge-
> able person and make good decisions because you will know all the
> bad and all the good about the situation.

Years of reading student papers make me certain that while this paper
was meant to be the final version of a multidraft assignment, Alicia
had dashed it off the night before. Having thirty-six students in the
class hampers me from checking that every piece in the process is in
place. Even with this caveat, I believe that Alicia and many other students like her would benefit from a carefully crafted prompt.

A team of researchers from the Educational Testing Service and
the National Writing Project reviewed classroom writing samples collected as part of the 1998 NAEP writing test in order to analyze the
state of writing instruction throughout the nation. Speaking at a June
26, 2001, roundtable discussion of their research at the Council of
Chief State School Officers' annual conference, Barbara Storms and
Claudia Gentile posited that constructing an assignment that elicits
good writing may be as difficult for teachers as writing the essays is for
their students. The research indicated that teachers must strike a balance between giving students too much and too little choice in writing prompts. The topics should engage students in complex thinking

and clearly indicate the intended audience for the piece of writing. In an in-depth study of writing samples, researchers discovered that "the quality of a teacher's assignment could determine the quality of students' writing" (Hoff 2001).

Joan and Craig Cotich, who are respectively a high school teacher and university instructor in Santa Barbara, California, have made an art of creating good writing prompts. Their analysis of the questions teachers typically ask provided me with insight into how to do a better job with this important piece of the puzzle. In an article for *California English*, they wrote:

> Without a prompt that clearly invites an argument and a developed support of that argument, students become confused about the "essay" and what it entails. A great prompt will not guarantee a great essay, but it will help students understand the kind of writing expected from them.
>
> Essays are difficult enough to write, and a good prompt will help students more clearly see the purpose of an assignment. As we analyzed teacher prompts for essays, we recognized some patterns in problematic essay prompts: they were often too long; they were assigned to test knowledge; they asked for a re-telling of a story; they did not ask for the development of a thesis; they asked too many questions; or they asked for description of plot, character, or setting.
>
> Below are two prompts that we analyzed and then revised.

Prompt No. 1

> Courage is a characteristic that is praised in *To Kill a Mockingbird*. How are different aspects of courage illustrated through different incidents in the novel? What different definitions of courage do we learn? What is your final definition of courage?

> This asks for a definition essay, in which students will explain how their conceptions of the word "courage" were re-defined or just slightly changed by Harper Lee's novel. As the question is now framed, though, students must follow a three-step process before arriving at the final demand of the essay.

The first question asks students to describe the different "aspects" of courage in the novel, and most likely, students will believe that this is their first task rather than a step in a process. Students, then, relate incidents in the story where courage is illustrated, but they do not incorporate this step into the other two. If students treated this single question as the essay question, they would come up with a thesis that focused on Harper Lee's conception of courage.

The next question builds on the first, in that the question is targeted more toward students than toward Harper Lee. It now asks for a more "objective" definition of courage, demonstrated by the use of the word "we." Students here come up with various definitions of courage, and these definitions do not necessarily refer back to the incidents in the novel where courage is illustrated. Students often do not see the relation between these first two questions, and this is partly because they are framed as separate questions that do not reference each other. These first two sentences could easily be combined so that the student clearly sees that each type of courage defined must be supported with evidence from the text.

We believe that the last question is the most important question because it asks students to arrive at a final definition of courage, assuming that Lee's novel has reformulated their initial definition of courage. This last question also presumes that students will contrast their initial definition of courage with their "final" definition of courage. But this final question shifts the focus from the "we" to the "you," and students may again view this shift as a call for a separate answer rather than for a unified answer.

Students treat this prompt as a three-part response, and they do not come up with a single thesis statement that incorporates all three questions into a single answer. To elicit a better response, we rewrote the prompt as seen below.

REWRITE: In *To Kill A Mockingbird*, Harper Lee reformulates (changes) the meaning of courage. How is courage redefined in the novel?

This single question captures the essence of the assignment—it asks students to recognize that Lee plays with and ultimately changes our conception of courage. Students are asked to state *how* courage is re-defined, and this will involve showing *how* the author does this.

Showing how, or illustrating how, the author does this involves bringing in examples from the text. Writing a Directive above the prompt such as "Incorporate examples from the novel to support your claims," will ensure that this is done.

Prompt No. 2

What is the significance of the title *To Kill a Mockingbird?* Choose two characters who represent "mockingbirds" in the novel and explain how they relate to the importance of the title. Use specific textual examples to show why each character is considered a "mockingbird." Which citizens of Maycomb learn lessons from these "mockingbirds," and what lessons do they learn?

Here is an example of a schizophrenic prompt. This prompt asks four different questions, and each of these could sustain an essay. The first question asks for an analysis of the title in relation to the text. This is a good question, but it is extremely general. Students can take this question in many different directions, depending on their interpretation of the novel. For teachers who do not want to read 20 papers that sound the same, this general prompt may be appealing. For those teachers looking for something more uniform, this prompt may not be the best choice.

The second question is much more specific in terms of direction. Students know they must choose two characters and then show how these characters "represent" mockingbirds. This demands a two-fold interpretation.

1. Students must first interpret the meaning of mockingbirds in the novel.
2. They must analyze two characters according to how well they conform to the characteristics or symbolism of the mockingbird. We believe that this question is the best of the three.

The third sentence is repetitive, since this guideline is already stated in the Directions. It is best to avoid writing rules or guidelines within the prompt itself, for this distracts students from the goal of the prompt: to clearly understand what is being asked of them.

The last sentence includes a third and fourth question. These last two questions are subordinate to the first two questions, but because these come last, students may interpret these last questions as the most important. Students will probably include parts of the last questions in answering either of the first two, but this prompt structure will confuse the reader.

REWRITE: Harper Lee uses the theme of "mockingbirds" throughout the novel. Choose two characters who best represent mockingbirds, and explain why these two characters are likened to mockingbirds.

Below is a prompt for you to analyze on your own. We have provided some criticism of the prompt, but try to critique the prompt on your own and see what you come up with.

Prompt No. 3

There are many contrasting definitions of what makes "good folks" in *To Kill a Mockingbird*. Choose three characters who have different definitions of what makes "good folks," and explain their opinions. What do you think is the author's message? What is *your* opinion about what makes "good folks"?

- The real thesis question is the last line. This question asks for three very different things in terms of how a student will answer them.
- The first command asks for an essay that could become a compare/contrast essay if the task is to analyze the similarities and differences between these different characters' conception of "good folks."
- The first question asks for the student to interpret the characters' feelings and thoughts about good folks, and this question presumably asks the student to interpret the author's intent.
- The second question is ambiguous. The author's message *when?*
- The last question is the best because it will involve (at least partially) answering all of the above questions.

I have begun asking myself the following questions whenever I write a prompt:

- Does the question invite reflection and analysis or have I simply asked students to retell the story?
- Does the prompt invite many possible responses or does there seem to be only one correct answer?
- Does the prompt send students back to the text for evidence?
- Have I indulged in my own multiple interpretations of the text and written so many questions that students have no idea where to begin?

The College Board's AP Language and AP Literature prompts offer excellent models. While they often need to be purged of literary terminology for younger or less academic students, these prompts have been carefully designed to elicit the kind of analysis that I believe all students are capable of writing.

It may seem an impossible task, but I often write personalized prompts for students. Knowing how much or how little guidance an individual student needs to get started, I craft each prompt with a particular writer in mind. This works better when students are writing on many different outside reading books rather than on a novel we are studying as a class because kids can't "shop" prompts and then make assumptions about how I view them as writers. Of course I save these seemingly one-of-a-kind prompts for future use. For Alicia's next essay, on My Ántonia, I wrote:

Specially Designed Prompt for Alicia Escalera on Willa Cather's My Ántonia

How did Ántonia and Jim's friendship lend focus to Cather's novel? Write an essay in which you explain how learning about one another helped both characters learn about themselves.

Not only did Alicia write a much more focused and cohesive essay on this novel than she did for *The Bell Jar*, but in June she chose the *My Ántonia* essay from her portfolio as an example of how she had grown as a writer over the course of the year. A luminous phrase from her essay still rings in my ears: "Jim and Ántonia help each other grow their separate ways together." Teachers of writing cannot assume that one method of getting started will work for all students. We have to take students where they are and provide the scaffolding they need to improve. Some will need more direction than others. We must help them grow their separate ways.

♎

TWO

Teaching Informational and Persuasive Writing

> The personal essay is, in my experience, a form of discovery.
> What one discovers in writing such essays is where one stands
> on complex issues, problems, questions, subjects. In writing the
> essay, one tests one's feelings, instincts, thoughts in the crucible
> of composition.
>
> —Joseph Epstein, introduction to *The Norton Book
> of Personal Essays*

It is difficult teaching students to write cohesive analytical essays because they haven't read much in the genre. Few seventh-grade students spend much time reading newspaper editorials or gravitate to a book with the title *Best Essays*. Science and social studies textbooks offer examples of informational (and sometimes deadly) prose, but where can students find models for the kinds of personal or persuasive essays that we so often assign? How can they develop the confidence of essayist Joseph Epstein when he tests his "feelings, instincts, thoughts in the crucible of composition" without a sense of what a well-crafted essay looks like?

Examples of excellent student writing can be useful models of cohesive prose, but young writers need to read professional essays to develop a feel for the genre. I have also found that most students lack the patience to listen to an "A" paper being read aloud. In some groups this can also be an uncomfortable moment for the writer who has been planted on the pedestal. Even posting outstanding essays (something I very much like doing) rarely inspires students to read one another's papers all the way through. Most often students simply check to see who made the board.

If students are to read essays, I need to incorporate this reading into my curriculum. Many state standards demand that students read "informational materials and workplace documents." Consequently, publishers have taken to including more and more nonfiction in their language arts anthologies. Often this has been done artfully: a fictional story followed by the newspaper article that inspired it or a paired essay and poem addressing the same theme. Creative textbook authors are saving teachers a great deal of research and time at the Xerox machine.

Reading Like a Writer

In his introduction to *The Best Essays 1999*, Edward Hoagland writes, "Essays are how we speak to one another in print—caroming thoughts not merely in order to convey a certain packet of information, but with a special edge or bounce of personal character in a kind of public letter" (1999, xiii). Hoagland believes that writers "catch the gist of what other people have also been feeling and clarify it for them" (xiii). Absolute originality of topic is not essential. Writers need only have a fresh interpretation of the subject, however familiar. To bring this lesson home to students, I have them read one of the following essays by accomplished writers on seemingly ordinary matters. All of them can be found in *The Best American Essays* (1995), edited by Robert Atwan:

- "Maintenance," in which Naomi Shihab Nye uses cleaning house as a metaphor
- "How to Get Out of a Locked Trunk" by Philip Weiss, which explores the feelings associated with being trapped in a relationship

- "Hair" by Marcia Aldrich, describing how the hairstyles of women in her family over time reflect personal identity
- "Silent Dancing" by Judith Ortiz Cofer, about childhood memories of her two very different parents
- "Mother Tongue," where Amy Tan explains the many different languages she speaks and how this influenced her novel *The Joy Luck Club*
- "No Wonder They Call Me a Bitch," an amusing essay by Ann Hodgman, who taste-tested dog food—herself!

I select model essays that focus on subjects students recognize. Choice is also extremely important to teenagers. Whatever collection you decide to use, be sure to let students choose from among a group of essays. For some, length will determine their choice, but that shouldn't matter if you know that the selection is uniformly excellent.

Putting students into groups according to the essay they read, I ask groups to see if they can identify the writer's thesis. I warn them that the thesis may not be a tidy sentence in the opening paragraph but might instead follow an attention-grabbing opening anecdote or even remain hidden until the very end of the essay. The essayist may take several sentences to state the key idea of the piece. What is important is the conversation that such a "find-the-thesis" task generates. I want students to negotiate among themselves what *is* the main idea of this essay and to discover that professional writers often do not state their thesis and three points of proof in the opening paragraph.

As I circulate among the groups and check that this first task has been accomplished, I ask students to identify the evidence the essayist has marshaled to support the thesis. I remind students that evidence can take many forms: statistics, anecdotes, or examples. Requiring each group to fill out the form in Figure 2–1 helps students stay focused. Typical teenagers need to be held accountable. Collecting these papers at the end of class helps them feel that I care about what has gone on inside their group and want to understand more fully the breadth of their discussion. In truth, I rarely have time to read these papers carefully.

Analyzing a Published Essay

Group members: _____

Title of essay: _____

Author: _____

Thesis statement: _____

_____

Evidence:

1. _____

_____

2. _____

_____

3. _____

_____

4. _____

_____

5. _____

_____

© 2002 by Carol Jago from *Cohesive Writing*. Portsmouth, NH: Heinemann.

FIGURE 2–1   *Analyzing a published essay*

Deconstructing What Professional Essayists Do

Once students have grasped that professional essayists approach their subjects from many different angles and with many different methods of elaboration, I want them to examine how essayists develop a line of thought. None of my students can imagine waking up and saying, "Gee, I'd like to write an essay this morning!" Many keep diaries or write stories and poems of their own volition, but none of them choose to write an essay just for fun. Essays are what teachers make you write.

When I ask students why they think anyone might choose to write an essay, they often have no idea. I share with them Joseph Epstein's (1997) comments about an essay he is looking forward to writing:

> I plan before long to write an essay on the subject of talent. Just now I know very little about the subject apart from the fact that it fascinates me. "We need a word between talent and genius," Valéry once said. He may well be correct, but just now I am myself not even clear on the precise definition of the word "talent." I know only that talent tends to be something magical, or at least confers magic on its possessors, no matter in what realm: art, athletics, crime. In this essay, I intend to speak of my own admiration for the talented, question the extent to which I may myself have any spark of talent, try to figure out the meaning of talent in the larger scheme of existence. Through this essay I hope to learn what I really think about this complex subject and, while doing so, to learn perhaps something new about myself and the world. (16)

The idea that one should approach the task of writing an essay without knowing exactly what you already think is a foreign concept to students. Reflecting on his essay "The Man in the Water" Roger Rosenblatt explained that:

> Often I will wait to write till the last possible minute before deadline, hoping not to solve a particular mystery, but to feel it more deeply. "The Man in the Water" was written in forty-five minutes, but I brooded about it for many days. Three full days that air crash

led the evening news. I came to believe that the man in the water was the reason, yet no one had said so because he had done something people could not understand. In too many ways the piece shows that it was written in forty-five minutes, but it resonated with readers at the time because it dwelt on the mystery of an act that people did not understand, or want to understand. Certain stories people do not want to understand. The mystery makes them feel closer to one another than would any solution. (12)

Rosenblatt is talking about his essay on the 1982 airplane disaster in Washington, D.C., when Air Florida flight 90 hit the Fourteenth Street Bridge on takeoff, killing seventy-eight people. One of the passengers who died passed a helicopter lifeline again and again to others in the water around him. *A Man in the Water*, Rosenblatt's collection of stories and essays, was published by Random House in 1994 and is available online at *<http://www.pbs.org/newshour/ww /rosenblatt.html>*.

I assure students that Epstein's and Rosenblatt's sense of self-exploration kept me writing an education column for our local newspaper, and later for the *Los Angeles Times*, for fifteen years. There were so many things that I saw in the classroom and in education that I wanted to think about more carefully. Writing helped me do this. I hand students copies of an essay I wrote about good manners in school. It was inspired by a news story about an odd piece of legislation mandating student respect. All I knew for sure when I sat down to write was that the idea of this law made me uneasy.

Yes, Ma'am. No, Sir

Louisiana Governor Mike Foster has recently sponsored a "Respect" bill that if passed would require students to say "yes, sir" and "no, ma'am" to their teachers. Thus far the bill has garnered considerable support passing the state Senate with a vote of 34–5. "The governor thought it was important that respect be shown in the schools to teachers," said Trey Williams, Mr. Foster's deputy press secretary. "Once you get respect back in the classroom, that's half the battle on discipline."

I agree. Students should address their teachers with respect. But the other half of the so-called battle will only ever be won when teachers demonstrate respect for students. Such respect takes many forms: starting class on time, having a clear lesson plan, returning student papers and tests in a timely manner, keeping a tidy classroom. Little things matter a great deal.

It also seems absurd to demand that students say "yes, ma'am" or "no, sir" to a classroom teacher outfitted in jeans and Nikes. Even in casual Southern California such sartorial habits send a subconscious message to children. They suggest that the business being conducted here is informal and laid-back. No need to put your best foot forward. Your teacher certainly didn't when preparing to meet you this morning.

Now kindergarten teachers who spend a lot of time on their knees have good reason to dress casually, but then sheer size establishes their ascendancy over 5-year-olds. High school teachers have no such advantage. Many of the bright young things entering the profession are only a few years older than their charges. Inevitably they struggle to establish their right to be in charge. And as many learn the hard way, without classroom control, it is not possible to teach.

One of the easiest ways for a young teacher struggling with discipline to merit respect is to put on a shirt and tie. Of course this teacher's character and content knowledge should carry more weight than his appearance, but until those become a natural part of his visage, he needs to wear the trappings of a professional. Ultimately respect will need to be earned, but formal attire at least deters disrespect.

I am reminded of the black and white habits the Dominican nuns who taught me at Queen of Peace High School wore. The mysterious garb had a lot to do with the respect they were able to elicit. I know it wasn't that we were any more naturally inclined to pay attention to our ninth grade English teacher than kids are today, but something about Sister Albert Mary demanded it. I think the wimple helped.

Legislating for respect will likely achieve nothing. One can only wonder how the Louisiana governor plans to punish 10-year-old offenders who refuse to parrot "Yes, sir. No, sir." Instead of passing another law, let's earn—by our teaching, by our character, by our dress—our students' respect.

by Carol Jago

I then ask students to write for five minutes on how they feel about the subject of respect between teachers and students. Having them write before initiating a class discussion helps them prepare and allows me to call on students other than the usual suspects for a response. I don't expect students to read what they have written, but simply to share what they are thinking. Even a few minutes of writing seems to help them marshal their thoughts. We talk for about twenty minutes—I purposely choose a subject that teenagers have strong opinions about—and then I pass out crayons.

Students' eyes perk up. "Great. The hard work is over for the day," they think. They are wrong of course, but I see no reason to disabuse them of any assumption that generates interest in the assignment. I then ask them to take out the yellow crayon and, after rereading the essay, to underline what they think was my thesis. Once they have located what they believe is my main idea, I ask them to take up the red crayon and underline my points of proof, then with a blue crayon highlight sentences they see as providing "analysis." (Color choices are entirely arbitrary.) When students have finished, I ask them to turn to a partner and compare the "coloring" of their essays. I want them to see that in many ways I didn't figure out what I really had to say about the subject of respect in school until my final paragraph. A good essay is organic. It grows with the writing. Experienced essayists introduce an idea, explore the idea in an organized and engaging fashion, then bring the subject to a conclusion.

Writing to Persuade

Every teacher has had the experience of sitting down with a struggling student and trying to help him choose a topic, only to end up supplying him with one that is unsatisfactory to both student and teacher. Part of the problem is that adolescents are afraid of any subject that might seem "uncool." They are also reluctant to expose too much of themselves. Consequently, students end up writing on dull, safe subjects. We may be asking too much of novice writers when we expect them to begin with a strongly held opinion. As E. M. Forster has said, "How can I know what I think until I see what I say." An alternative approach is to design a lesson that invites students to explore a host of possible topics for possible use in a persuasive essay. Any newspaper offers hundreds of ideas.

Give each student a copy of a newspaper and ask them to scan the headlines for news stories that pique their interest. Have them clip these articles and save them for future reference. (Newspaper companies are keen to capture the next generation of readers. So worried are they about being rendered obsolete by the Internet that most will donate a week's worth of copies for classroom use.) Don't limit students to stories from the front page. If news of a sports team's loss or a rock star's arrest attracts them, say, "Cut it out." This part of the process usually takes a full class period because each student should have at least five stories to choose from.

The next day's lesson requires some planning. You may want to present students with an editorial on a recent news story. Remember, local issues often resonate with students more than national ones, though national tragedies always have currency. Foreign affairs generally fail to produce much response. Find an editorial subject about which your students have some background knowledge. Then work backward and find the news story the opinion piece is reacting to. I make copies of both and after we have read them we complete a chart together (see Figure 2–2).

Most standards and assessment instruments require students to be able to generate both informative (sometimes referred to as expository) and persuasive writing. It is essential that students learn to distinguish between the two. Here is how NAEP defines them:

Informational writing
Informative writing focuses primarily on the subject-matter element in communication. This type of writing is used to share knowledge

News Story	Opinion Piece
• Offers who, what, where, when, how • Full of facts • Authoritative tone, believable • Informs rather than persuades • Includes quotations • No opinion offered	• A response to an event or decision • Cites carefully chosen facts as evidence • Believable • Persuasive tone • Attempts to convince reader to think as the writer does • May contain call to action

FIGURE 2–2 *Informational and persuasive writing compared*

and to convey messages, instructions, and ideas. Informative writing may also involve reporting on events or experiences, or analyzing concepts and relationships, including developing hypotheses and generalizations.

Persuasive writing

Persuasive writing emphasizes the reader. Its primary aim is to influence others to take some action or to bring about change. Persuasive writing may contain great amounts of information—facts, details, examples, comparisons, statistics, or anecdotes—but its main purpose is not simply to inform but to persuade. This type of writing involves a clear awareness of what arguments might most affect the audience being addressed.

Comparing a news story with an editorial on the same subject is a good way to help students grasp the fundamental difference between these two types of writing.

Next, have students take one of the news stories they found intriguing and write an opinion piece in response. André, an avid basketball-playing ninth grader, chose an article from the sports section about the feud between Kobe Bryant and Shaquille O'Neal during the Lakers' 2001 season (before the team went on to win the championship). André cared a great deal about the Lakers' success and felt that the two players should declare a truce for the good of the team and the fans. At first he couldn't believe that this would be an appropriate topic for a persuasive essay. I assured him that it would and suggested that it might help him keep his persuasive intent at the forefront of his mind if he framed the essay as a letter to the players themselves. Using facts from a January 12, 2001, news story titled "O'Neal Was Frustrated Enough to Seek Trade" by *Times* staff writer Tim Brown as well as his own knowledge of the ongoing argument, André drafted the following letter.

Dear Mr. Bryant and Mr. O'Neal,

I am a life-long fan of the Lakers who is very upset by the way your problems are affecting the team. The newspapers say a lot of things including that you are both thinking of leaving L.A. This would be a tragedy for our city as well as for me personally. You guys are my heroes.

I have watched your games and can see that the two of you are not getting along well. According to an article I read one of your teammates called the feud "juvenile, all juvenile." That's what I think, too. Although I am only 14 years old, I know that my team comes first. Even when I'm mad at another player for slacking off or not passing to me, I still have to play my best. Maybe it sounds funny coming from a kid, but I think you should both grow up.

The Lakers need you both. Think about how great it felt when we won the championship last year. It could happen again if you guys could put this stuff behind you and just play ball.

Your fan,
André Cooper

André's letter captured the spirit of persuasive writing. The next step was to look at the NAEP characteristics of effective persuasive essays and help André see how he might improve what he had written.

General Characteristics of Writing by Mode: Persuasive

- understands the persuasive purpose
- takes and retains a position

- supports and develops a position through examples, details, statistics, and supporting evidence
- has coherent and logical organization
- gives attention to audience
- uses language level appropriate to the topic and voice desired by the writing
- demonstrates control of mechanics

Believing that ten minutes spent with a student writer on a draft in a short writing conference is worth an hour spent correcting their final copy, André and I put our heads together over this paper.

Ms. Jago: Looking at this list, what do you think you've done well in your draft, André?

André: Well, I think I definitely do the first two. I mean, I think I am really clear about how I feel. Spell check helped me with the spelling so I think I'm OK on the mechanics, too.

Ms. Jago: I agree. You state your position clearly and convey how much you care. What about supporting evidence? Was there anything else in that news story that you might have used to back up your main idea?

André: Well there was this one other part where Phil Jackson the coach was quoted.

Ms. Jago: Show me. [André pointed to a section of the news story that he had highlighted where the coach Phil Jackson weighed in on the controversy.]

André: I guess I could include that because Jackson says the same thing I do about the players needing to get over it.

Ms. Jago: What about the language level? Do you think calling Kobe and Shaq "you guys" fits with the tone of your letter? I mean you begin by addressing them as Mr. Bryant and Mr. O'Neal and then go on to tell them to "grow up." What is powerful to me about this letter is the way you try to shame them into seeing that a high school basketball player knows better than to behave this way. If that's your position, you want to sound mature.

André: I'll think about that.

Ms. Jago: Is there anything else that might make this letter more persuasive to your audience?

André: Well, maybe I could talk about how beautiful it is when Kobe and Shaq play in sync. I mean, it's magic.

Ms. Jago: I think that's a great idea. It would offer a really concrete alternative to what is happening at the moment on the court. I also think you should also consider sending this letter to the Laker office. We could look up their address in the phone book. Who knows? It might make a difference.

André: Would you read it again before I do?

Ms. Jago: You bet.

Most students' persuasive essays did not generate products as authentic as André's, but they were much improved over the kinds of essays I had received in the past. (André received a form-letter response on Laker letterhead. He framed it.) The difference seemed to be the time spent looking at real essays and thinking about what it meant to be an "essayist." It is possible to bully students into doing what is required, but the work that emerges is rarely very good. To produce good work, students need to care about their subject and have a reason to get it right. For some, a grade is enough of a reason. For others, only intrinsic value will do.

The 1998 NAEP eighth-grade persuasive writing prompt offers a good example of a writing situation that has intrinsic value for students:

Eighth-Grade Persuasive Prompt: Lengthening the School Year
Many people think that students are not learning enough in school. They want to shorten most school vacations and make students

spend more of the year in school. Other people think that lengthening the school year and shortening vacations is a bad idea because students use their vacations to learn important things outside of school.

What do you think?

Write a letter to your school board either in favor of or against lengthening the school year. Give specific reasons to support your opinion that will convince the school board to agree with you.

The following student response to this persuasive prompt was used as an exemplar of an advanced paper. Each paragraph is clearly organized and builds support for the student's point of view. It is a convincing analysis. This eighth-grade writer also employs the rhetorical strategies of irony and refutation of an opposing argument.

To Whom It May Concern,

I've heard about the debate of whether or not to lengthen the school year. I decided to voice my opinion. I believe that the school year should *not* be lengthened. Kids are stressed out enough with homework and school without adding more. Some might say that kids aren't learning enough, and since the future of the nation rests on their shoulders they need to go to school longer and learn more. I say those who are adults now went to school the same amount, if not shorter, of time that we do and they haven't completely ruined the country.

To make the country better you don't just need to know math, English, and, history; you need to know social skills like getting along with others. You learn social skills at school but you can learn them just as easily while on vacation. If you go to another country for vacation you learn to accept and respect other cultures.

This can help extinguish predujuces.

If you add more schoolwork and homework kids will get more stressed out. When you're stressed out you aren't as agreeable and sometimes just give up trying and don't care a difference in the world.

I once heard someone say that you are only a kid for a short time. When you're an adult you have enough stress and hardly any time for fun, so why put stress on kids and make them lose their time for fun. Why turn them into adults before their time?

I completely agree with the person who said this. Let kids have fun and not be stuck in a hot school listening to a lecture, or at home doing homework when they used to be swimming or hanging out with their friends.

Thank you for considering my letter. (U.S. Dept. of Education 1999, 44)

This persuasive essay was rated "Excellent" and received the top score of six on NAEP's six-point scoring guide. The twelfth-grade NAEP persuasive writing prompt was similarly designed to raise an issue that would seem authentic to student writers.

Twelfth-Grade Persuasive Prompt: One Vote

Your school is sponsoring a voter registration drive for 18-year-old high school students. You and three of your friends are talking about the project. Your friends say the following.

Friend 1: I'm working on the young voters' registration drive. Are you going to come to it and register? You're all 18, so you can do it. We're trying to help increase the number of young people who vote and it shouldn't be too hard—I read that the percentage of 18- to 20-year-olds who vote increased in recent years. We want that percentage to keep going up.

Friend 2: I'll be there. People should vote as soon as they turn 18. It's one of the responsibilities of living in a democracy.

Friend 3: I don't know if people should even bother to register. One vote in an election isn't going to change anything.

Do you agree with friend 2 or 3? Write a response to your friends in which you explain whether you will or will not register to vote. Be sure to explain why and support your position with examples from your reading experience. Try to convince the friend with whom you disagree that your position is the right one.

I was struck by the volume of reading this prompt demanded of twelfth-grade students before they could begin to write. You can download the entire 1999 NAEP *Writing Report Card* with other student exemplars and all their rubrics from *<http://nces.ed.gov/nationsreportcard/writing/>*.

The term *essay* comes from the French word *essai*, meaning to attempt, try, or experiment. Whatever the results of their attempts to persuade, I let students know that I will never stop expecting them to *essayer*, to try.

THREE

Ω

Teaching Narrative Writing

The following short story, written by a sixteen-year-old student, reflects both the best and the worst aspects of student work in the narrative mode.

This is powerful writing on a subject the student cares a great deal about. Her story is beautifully developed and went through multidrafts that the student was eager to share with her friends and her teachers for feedback, and writing this provided a vehicle for exploring her feelings.

Conversely, reading about suicide and teenage depression can mean a student is in trouble. The story is long, very long. If every one of the thirty-six students in this class had written at such length, I would be overwhelmed. Offering constructive criticism on a piece of writing so close to a student's heart is like navigating a minefield.

The Signs

I have had friends who had friends who committed suicide, but this was the extent of my experience with the whole thing. In the midst of it all, I never thought I could fall into such a category. I mean, I see my friends every day, but I can never tell what they're thinking. I never thought that I would be the friend of a friend who committed suicide.

Yet here I am.

I'm standing in the graveyard that's six blocks from my house, thirteen blocks from my high school, and nineteen blocks away from my former friend's house. I'm surrounded by friends from my high school who are crying because their friend committed suicide. Also among the people around me, there are the ones who are crying because a member of their family has committed suicide. One person, and this is the wake she left behind.

I'm angry, you know? Part of me is angry with myself because there had to have been signs, and I missed them. There has to be at least one thing that I missed, something that could have told me what she was going through, something that I should have picked up on, but didn't. I didn't, so she's gone.

But I'm angry with her also. She made this decision without talking to me or to anyone else first. She decided to take her life into her own hands, and this is what happened. I think about why she did this, about those signs I missed, signs that could have confessed a reason, but I can't find anything. There were so many options that she could have chosen, but this is what happened. I don't understand. She was always a fighter, but now all that's left of her is in a box on my shoulder.

I've been thinking a lot lately. I've been thinking about the past week or so before she died, just recent days when I saw her. We were hanging out together with our friends, laughing and talking. I don't remember anything being wrong then. I don't remember any signs.

"I hate getting tests back," Sarah lamented as we walked down the pathway toward our next class. I took the history test from her hand and looked it over. Her B– was better than my D so I really couldn't tell what it was that she was whining about. I rolled my eyes and handed it back.

"Yeah, you're a real idiot there, Sarah," I told her. She looked dejectedly at her feet and nodded. Joey shoved me aside and put an arm around Sarah's shoulder. Joey has always been the counselor among us.

"Don't listen to him. He's a doofus, and he's just jealous cause he's a micrometer above failing that class, and you're not," she said. "You're not an idiot, Sarah. You're smarter than the lot of us."

"Except you," Sarah reminded her. Joey shrugged.

"I bribe the teachers, but that doesn't matter," she pauses. I laugh and Sarah just smiles. "What matters is that you're smart and he's not," she finishes with a dramatic point to me. I swat at her hand and shake my head.

"I feel like an idiot though. I mean, a B minus is not going to be good enough for my dad. He's always yelling at me these days. In the meantime, I'm the only junior in this school who has never been on a date," Sarah said softly.

"That's not true," Joey volunteered as she shoved her hands into her pockets. *"I've never been on one."*

"Freaks don't count," I pointed out. Joey stuck her tongue out at me. I smirked and tried to pinch at it. She snipped her teeth at me and I backed off. Sarah smiled weakly and then just looked off into the distance. Joey pushed me away and then looked at Sarah again.

"Hey, what about Michael?" She asked. Sarah sighed and then shook her head.

"Michael doesn't care about me, and besides, the way I hear it, he's a commitment phobe," she responded.

"I thought you were looking for a date, not a fiancé," I teased. Joey threw her empty coke bottle at my head.

"Don't listen to Tom. Men are naturally insensitive. You know that," she reassured Sarah. Sarah smiled again.

"You're both insane," I called as I started up the stairs.

"That's why you love us," Joey called back before disappearing down the hallway with Sarah at her side. I chuckled and trotted up into the building. It was just another day. Sarah whining, Joey playing counselor and me just not caring.

I should have cared.

There are so many things that can drive a teenager crazy. There are so many problems that we face every day. There's school, and other teenagers, and parents, siblings, other people in the world . . . There are all sorts of things that we face all the time. But I faced them right along with her, and I never even thought of doing anything like this. Why would *anyone* slit their wrists?

It's still a little early in the morning. The sun is only slightly above the trees. The grass is fresh, illuminated in a vibrant green color and traced with bits of glistening morning dew. It seems almost fitting. She always loved the outdoors, the wonders of nature and all that it could produce.

As we walk down the pathway, this heavy box on our shoulders, I can hear her father whispering in Latin. I never knew that he spoke Latin. I'm not surprised though. He's a smart guy, a lawyer. Someone once told me all lawyers knew Latin, don't ask me where they got that from. I can think of a few lawyers who don't even know what 'carpe diem' means.

She used to tell lawyer jokes. "How many lawyers does it take to change a light bulb? Well, how many can you afford?" or better yet "Fifty four. Eight to argue, one to get a continuance, one to object, one to demur, two to research precedents, one to dictate a letter, one to stipulate, five to turn in their time sheets, two to depose, one to write interrogatories, two to settle, one to order a secretary to change the bulb, and twenty-eight to bill for professional services."

I'm surprised I remembered all that. I suppose that's something about her that I'll always remember then. This has got to be like one of those things where something is burned into your brain by trauma or something. Having a friend commit suicide is pretty traumatic.

I'm not the only one though. There was a whole group of us. She called it our circle of friends. Michael is to the side of me, and I think he's crying. I've never known him to cry before. What's sad is that I can't even bring myself to cry.

I think I'm too angry.

We put the box down. The little robed man stands up and opens his little black book. His dark eyes gaze across this sad crowd of ours.

"We are gathered today . . ." What does he know?

"Michael, I think your girlfriend is depressed!" Joey called. Sarah glared at our mutual friend and tried to bury her face into her thick history book. We were sitting on the green hill in the middle of our school eating lunch. Across the way, Michael the big jock was chatting with his jock friends when Joey had called. Michael was a big guy, and some people were scared of him, but they were wrong. He was a nice guy, always friendly and always open-minded.

He also loved Sarah dearly. As much as a male teenager could love a female teenager anyway. When Joey called, he looked over at us, smiled and then excused himself so that he could join us. Sarah blushed and tried to pretend like she was studying Maoist China. We all knew better.

"I'm not his girlfriend," she hissed softly to Joey without looking up.

"Then why is he coming over here?" I teased. Michael and Sarah were very different, and yet they were perfect together.

"Hello, Sarah," Michael said as he sat down next to her.

"Hello, Michael," *she replied innocently. I glanced at them with a smirk and then noticed that Joey was smiling at them happily. I suppose she always was a hopeless romantic. I never really much paid attention to it, you know, the mating habits of other human beings. There are more important things, like video games.*

"Sarah, would you do me the honor of going out with me on Friday?" *Michael asked in a soft tone. I wondered then if Joey had been coaching him. Sarah must have wondered this too for she shot Joey a look before looking at Michael.*

"I'm sorry. I can't. I have to study for the history test," *she replied.*

"Study on Saturday," *Joey suggested.*

"Yeah, we can have a study group, just the four of us," *I suggested.*

"I could probably use it. Lord knows, Tom could," *Joey added. I rolled my eyes and glared at her. She stuck her tongue out at me. Sarah sighed and looked at her book again. There was a lost look in her eyes.*

"Maybe," *she consented softly. I could never figure out why she avoided Michael like the plague. Maybe she was afraid of him. He grinned though.*

"So, maybe I could pick you up at seven?" *He asked. Sarah smiled very weakly.*

"Maybe."

"Ashes to ashes, dust to dust," the robed man says.

She's not ashes. She's not dust. She's a body, robbed of life, blood drained from the veins in her wrist. All that is in that box is the remnants of a person that was. A person full of energy and hopes for the future, energy and hopes that slowly drained away after the years. Why? Why couldn't I see it?

The sun is a little higher now. It's being reflected off the shiny finish of the coffin as it's being lowered into the ground. The fresh grass has been dug up and replaced by disheveled mud. The air is filled with the smell of the fresh dirt that has been dug up like the past by a shovel that sank six feet deep.

I see her mother, resting in her husband's arms and crying as she watches the machine lower her daughter into the earth, apparently the place where she came from originally according to the robed man. So the grieved parents stand in each other's arms and say goodbye with silent tears. He's still muttering in Latin.

It occurs to me that neither of them understands this either.

I'm standing here, watching as people who barely knew her walk by and pay their respects. Suddenly I can't help but think of the time when we were in middle school, in a humanities class, and the topic of the day was teen suicide. The teacher was talking about the reasons teens committed suicide, reactions from people close to them, etc. I remember wondering where he got that information from. How did he know why they had committed suicide? How did he know how people reacted to the whole thing?

She had raised her hand and asked how any body could be so selfish. The teacher had replied that when someone is in a state such that they will even consider committing suicide, he or she would either believe that no one would care about his or her death, or that he or she just can't think about anyone else.

I don't think I could believe either of those things about her. I don't believe she could ever believe that no one would care, and I could never believe that she wouldn't care about anyone else.

I don't know how she could.

The diner wasn't too crowded as we settled into the booth. This was good because Joey and Sarah hated loud places. I sat next to Joey and Michael slid in and made himself comfortable next to Sarah.

"We're all quiet this evening," Joey pointed out. "Maybe we could break out into song," she suggested with a grin. I rolled my eyes.

"You're weird," I said.

"You're a jerk," she replied evenly.

"Guys," Sarah warned us softly.

"Seriously, I mean, we need to relax a little here," Joey said. "We need to sing, we need to dance—"

"We ain't in France," I interrupted.

"Whatever you say, Lumiere," she teased. There's a pause. "Got it."

"Uh, oh," Michael says.

"When met with the grace and the fury we face," Joey starts softly singing her favorite song. "Some people turn and run away. Is that the way to live?"

"Together we can find, a way not to fall behind," Michael joins in. He doesn't have a bad voice either. "A way to know what to say. Can't we just learn to give?"

"So here we are, we're waiting to see," they started singing together. "It's time for the choosing, which one will it be?"

"God, not country music," Sarah lamented. Joey chuckled and nudged her across the table.

"Have a little spirit, kiddo," she said. Then she pretended to drum the table. "Now we don't have to be alone," she sang. "You don't have to go through on your own."

"Together we fight to the end," Michael and I both joined in. "Together we will find a way. It can't be enough just to stagger along. If life is too boring, then we're doing it wrong. This is why we're friends. This is how we have our say."

"Could you guys be quiet?" Sarah asked, her face turning slightly red. Those few other patrons in the diner were looking at our table, but there were nothing but smiles all around as we sang our song of inspiration.

"If we want our own paradise," Joey prompted Michael.

"Before we can choose," Michael turned to me.

"We must think twice," I chorused.

"So which one will it be?" we three sang together. Suddenly Sarah slammed her fists down on the table, silencing us.

"Just stop it, okay? You're embarrassing me," she said with the appearance of tears in her eyes before she rose to her feet and ran over Michael's feet to the bathroom. Joey paused to look at me, then at Michael, then at me again. Finally, she sighed and I let her out to go follow our friend. After she left, we were silent.

"I wish Sarah weren't like that," Michael confessed finally. "I love her, ya know, but she's so volatile. I don't know what's going to set her off next."

"I don't know. Maybe there's something going on with her dad again," I suggested. "She hasn't been feeling that great lately, I think."

"You think she might be sick?" Michael asked, his tone slightly worried.

"I don't know. I'm not a doctor, nor do I want to become one," I replied with a weak smirk. He smiled back and nodded. I nodded back and then looked toward the bathroom. I was sure that Joey could handle whatever was going on with Sarah, but still, I was starting to get worried.

"So here we are, waiting to see. Which one will it be?"

That's what I wrote on the note that I dropped into her grave.

That's the question that's burning in my mind. This is the choice that she made. Why?

I still can't believe how I missed the signs. I was her best friend. I was supposed to be able to see those things. I was supposed to see into her mind when she was depressed, into her heart when she was suicidal. Why couldn't she have talked to me about this? Isn't that what I'm for? To talk to?

I feel so blind. In the end, I didn't see the signs. No one did. That's why we're all standing here, tears in our eyes, the sun on backs, surprise and grief in our hearts as people start to throw pieces of dirt and dying roses, roses that began to die as soon as they were plucked, into the fresh grave.

Not one of us saw any signs at all.

Not me, not her father, not her mother, not Michael, and strangely enough, though she was the one who talked to her the most, not even Sarah saw it. It just happened one day out of the blue. It was just another phone call, I had thought, but now, it was a strange message that no one could believe. How could it happen?

I sat down on my bed and pulled out my English reading book. Joey was supposed to call me twenty minutes ago, and yet the phone hasn't rung. Finally it did and I grabbed it enthusiastically.

"Joey, you're late," I said playfully into the line. The first response that I got was a soft sob and then a voice finally spoke.

"Tom, sweetie," Joey's mother, Mrs. Hathaway, had said, her voice weak. "It's about Joey."

Now it's my turn. I pick up a small handful of dirt that feels soft in my fingers; it feels like it's trying to escape my hand. I toss it on to the polished dark wood of her coffin. I can hear the dirt land with a soft thump before it spreads across the grooves. With that, I force myself to walk away.

I didn't see the signs.

I didn't know she wanted a boyfriend.

"I'm the only junior in this school who has never been on a date," Sarah said softly.

"That's not true," Joey volunteered as she shoved her hands into her pockets. "I've never been on one."

I didn't know that her parents were never home, that her father the lawyer workaholic was never around.

"How many lawyers does it take to change a light bulb? Well, how many can you afford?"

I didn't know she had the highest grades in our class, and that she was studying into overkill just to get them.

"Yeah, we can have a study group, just the four of us," I suggested.
"I could probably use it. Lord knows, Tom could," Joey added.

I didn't know that she hated playing counselor to everyone else in her life.

Joey has always been the counselor among us.

I didn't know that she had no idea what she was going to do with her life and that it scared her.

None of us knew until it was too late. We didn't know until we read the note that she left behind. Why? She walked away from me after all this, away from us, away from this world that had embraced her more than she must have realized.

Sarah throws another piece of dirt on to the coffin, and again the sound radiates through me. Make the sounds stop. I just want them to stop. A tear falls down her cheek as she sobs again and leans back into Michael's grasp. I can't look, so I turn away.

The sun is a little higher now. It just goes to show me then. She told me once that even when the sun sets, it rises again the next day. There's always a future, even after the past. Why couldn't she have remembered that?

I don't suppose I'll ever understand.

I gaze up at the sun and I wonder if maybe it's a sign. Maybe it's her way of telling me that everything's going to be okay, like a message from beyond or something, if you believe in that sort of thing. The sun set yesterday, but it rose again today. It's got to mean something.

I just don't know if that makes it a sign.

The End

by Claire Bennett

Claire had this to say about her story:

Reflection on "The Signs"

I have worked harder on this story than I ever have worked on a story in my life. I wrote, edited, rewrote, edited some more, until I finally had something that I was satisfied with. It was important to me in a sort of therapeutic way. It was a way to remind myself that there are people around me who would wonder about "the signs" that they missed, just like the main character of this story. It was a way to remind myself that even though people don't always show it, they do care. To be honest, I was trying to tell myself why I couldn't make the decision I was thinking about making. I believe that this story is very much a part of me. It's the first story that I have ever really written from some place deep inside myself. I'm proud of the story because it seemed for the first time that I managed to get down on paper exactly what I wanted to. With most stories that I have written, I come up with all sorts of different ways to write certain events in my head, but in the end I have to choose just one and it never feels right. Things were different with this story. I reread the final draft and I actually felt satisfied. I gave it to friends and teachers to read, and every single one showed me an emotional reaction, and those reactions communicated to me just how well I had done with the story. That is what I'm truly pleased with.

The Good, the Bad, and the Worrisome

Claire's story exemplifies my dilemma with teaching narrative writing. Like the Colorado students at the Uncensored Conference, many of my students are hungry for more opportunities to write creative fiction, yet I can't help but worry that I invite disaster with such assignments. Students love writing "trauma" stories. How do I know what is true and what is made up? Sometimes the line between the two can be hard to discern even for the student writer. Most states have laws that require teachers to report evidence of child abuse, and the recent spate of school shootings has put several teachers in difficult positions for not reporting evidence of violent behavior in student journals and creative writing. No wonder many English teachers are shying away from creative writing.

In *Bodily Discourse: When Students Write About Abuse and Eating Disorders*, Michele Payne goes beyond the concerns about how to respond and grade such writing and explores the reasons why students choose to write about such troubling subjects.

> Students may write about their experiences with bodily violence in part because strangers—within the impersonal nature of public spaces—have been constructed within American emotional culture as safe spaces to express emotional intensity and lack of emotional control. Although many writing teachers assume the student wants a therapeutic relationship with them, some students may be counting on a well-defined boundary between writing teacher and therapist. Students may not expect a response on the feeling level from a teacher because that would contradict the prevailing emotional standards. (2000, 18)

Payne builds an argument for listening "to the words of students as they make and unmake themselves; write and rewrite culture; consider and reconsider language, power, and truth" (xxvi). She recommends that teachers focus on responding to the student's writing rather than to the content, warning against the impulse to read student texts through a psychotherapeutic lens. As every public school teacher knows, there are circumstances where one must act for fear of a student's safety. However, Payne found that what most students want from their writing teacher is help with craft.

Narrative Standards

For all its potential to inspire worrisome products, narrative writing is a common requirement in most state standards documents. Wisconsin's Model Academic Standards for English Language Arts demand that eighth graders be able to "write a narrative based on experience that uses descriptive language and detail effectively, presents a sequence of events, and reveals a theme" as well as "write creative fiction that includes major and minor characters, a coherent plot, effective imagery, descriptive language, and concrete detail." To help students meet these standards, teachers must teach students how to:

- create major and minor characters;
- define a setting;
- order events;
- develop a plot line;
- generate narrative movement; and
- use dialogue.

The kinds of prompts most often used to measure students' mastery of these elements of narration often read something like, "write an article for a sports magazine telling the story of a time when you participated in a hobby or skill you enjoyed" or "write a letter to a friend telling the story of a time you had to make an important decision." While these prompts may work well for state or national assessments, they are not questions I would choose to use in my classroom.

Teaching Narration Piecemeal

I teach narration piecemeal, inviting students to experiment with the essential aspects of narration through short exercises. These low-stakes writing tasks help students build the writing muscles needed to write stories. Just as an athlete goes through a set of warm-up exercises before a game or any dancer stretches before a performance, so writers must develop both strength and flexibility before they can write effectively. All of these writing exercises are completed in class under timed conditions. I want students to work fast, scribbling away, unworried about producing something "good," playing with the task I have set before them. In his essay "A Way of Writing," William Stafford explains that in order to write well,

> I must be willing to fail. If I am to keep on writing, I cannot bother to insist on high standards. I must get into action and not let anything stop me, or even slow me much . . . Later others—and maybe

I myself—will make judgments. Now, I am headlong to discover.
(1978, 18)

I want students to be "headlong to discover" what it feels like to create characters and then make them speak. I want them to construct fictional worlds and discover as they write what their characters find themselves doing in these worlds. I want them to play with ideas.

Bringing Characters to Life

To help students explore the inner lives of fictional characters I have them write short interior monologues for three characters, each of whom has just met the boy, girl, man, woman of his or her dreams.

The three characters are

- a fourteen-year-old, mall-loving, ditsy girl;
- a forty-year-old postal clerk who lives with his mother; and
- a ninety-year-old widow living in a retirement home.

I assign each character separately, inviting students to imagine what it would be like to be this character. The interior monologue should focus on the things that matter most to this person. The more concrete the examples and imagery the better. The postal clerk may be fantasizing that the brown-haired girl standing in line will make a sensitive choice of stamps. The geriatric lover may have just received a wink from the man of her dreams as he staggered down the hall in his walker. I give students about seven to eight minutes for each stint of writing. We stop to hear a few monologues as the lesson proceeds. The actors in the class love to ham up their readings. This is also a perfect St. Valentine's Day lesson.

Creating a Setting

Often our memories of a place are triggered by smells. Before class I prepare three boxes full of cotton balls, enough in each for every student in the class. One set I spray with a disinfectant, any household cleaner will do. Another I spray with cheap perfume. A third I spray with air freshener. Again working one at a time through the scents, I hand around the treated cotton balls and then ask students to construct a setting that this smell brings to mind. They must describe the place—the time of day and time of year—as well as the sensations stimulated by being in this place. Be sure to do this on a day when the weather will permit opening the windows. One of the best things about this lesson is that students can't quite believe that you are asking them to write based on a smell. It opens their eyes to the power of scent to evoke time and place.

Point of View

This exercise is one I adapted from John Gardner's *The Art of Fiction: Notes on Craft for Young Writers* (1991). This book is filled with wonderful writing assignments—Gardner was a masterful creative writing teacher as well as a novelist—but I find that the tasks often need a level of scaffolding for middle and high school students. First, ask students to imagine a scene they know well. (As our school is six blocks from the ocean, most of my students choose the beach.) Then ask them to choose a character from the following list and describe the setting from the character's perspective, without mentioning what has just happened in this character's life:

- an old woman whose mean and nasty husband has just died;
- a young man who has just committed a crime;
- a middle-aged grocery store clerk who has just won the lottery; and, if you think your students can handle it,
- a teenager waiting for the results of an AIDS test.

Ordering Events

One way to give students practice with ordering events in a story is to offer them a series of story starters that cry out for "What happens next?" As in the previous exercises, I have students approach each prompt separately. This helps keep them on task as well as allows me to judge when one starter falls flat and to move on to the next one more quickly.

- You are sitting in your room listening to music when suddenly the ceiling, walls, and floor begin growing hair . . .
- You are dozing through math class when all at once the teacher begins to bark . . .
- You climb into your friend's car only to discover that the backseat is full of frogs . . .
- You are trying to study for a history test when suddenly Napoleon/Queen Victoria/George Washington/Marco Polo starts talking to you . . .

Writing Dialogue

Show students an art print (posters, slides, and color transparencies all work fine) in which there are two or more figures. It doesn't matter whether the figures are small or large, in the foreground or background. Ask students to give the two characters names and then to write a dialogue between the two characters. Each one must speak at least six times. Such arbitrary rules help students believe that what we are doing is serious work. I give students about eight minutes to complete the exercise and then ask if anyone would be willing to share their dialogue. Typically we hear a few—and they are often wildly different—and then I show them another picture. We do this three or four times and then just when they think they've mastered the concept, I show them a picture with two animals and have them write this dialogue. It's a delightful way to end class.

My only stipulation is that students try their hands at each of the exercises. Apart from the acclaim of classmates when a student reads a particularly creative piece or my on-the-spot response, students receive no evaluation of these papers. The assignment is entirely credit/no credit. I want to give students the freedom to write creatively without fear of failure, headlong to discover.

Autobiographical Narration—The Dread College Essay

Strong narrative writing can be a powerful tool for helping bring dry college essays come to life. Every October, high school seniors panic.

Without further procrastination and with much ado, the time has come for them to write the dread college essay. What students find most terrifying about this portion of their application is the enormous latitude that colleges offer in terms of what students can write about. Though the wording of prompts differs from campus to campus, applicants are essentially instructed to "Tell us about you."

Can you imagine having to craft 500–600 words on the subject of "you" without freezing up? It doesn't help that teachers have done such a good job of making students aware how important it is to consider the specific audience for any piece of writing. The more aware seventeen-year-olds are of this audience, who holds in its hands the next four years of their lives, the more terrified teenagers become. The first thing anyone writing a college essay needs to do is CALM DOWN.

My students wail, "But I'm just a regular person." "We go to Hawaii for vacation. How can I write about that?" "Karina is so lucky. Her sister was in a terrible accident." "Nothing ever happened to me." Instead of responding to this whining (which is in fact a genuine call for help), I ask students to take out a piece of paper and create a time line of their lives. Recalling accidents, trips, calamities, triumphs, milestones and mishaps, good times and bad, inevitably triggers all kind of memories. I then ask students to think about what they want to reveal about themselves in a college essay. To help them, I have them put their names in the middle of blank sheet of paper and surround the name with words they feel best describe them, both strengths and weaknesses.

Then I ask students to highlight one or two qualities as the key characteristics they want to focus on in their essay. Once they decide, they can then choose a story that illuminates this quality. For example, if what a student thinks is important to communicate is determination, a story about coming back from an injury might be appropriate. For a student who wants to convey loyalty, a story about sticking with a team even when they were losing might be the best choice. What is so effective about having created the time line first is that if the essay on loyalty stalls, the writer can abandon it without quite starting all over. The time line will show if there are other stories that might work better. The cluster of descriptive words will offer suggestions of other character traits that might be more important to reveal. Maybe that story about sticking with the team was really about the power of friendship. Or maybe the story is about overcoming a character flaw.

Striking a balance between simple storytelling and demonstrating insight into themselves can be difficult for students. I always tell them not to worry about length while they are writing the story, to write all the details down including dialogue and minute description of setting. They can figure out how to trim later, picking and choosing details that illuminate the quality they want to showcase. Whatever narrative subject they eventually choose to write about—that one night, my trip to Israel, being cut from the cross-country team, the death of a beloved grandparent, falling out of a car—students will want the story to illuminate these key qualities.

Before beginning their first drafts, I warn of common dangers:

- Listing information that appears elsewhere in the application: If a student has made the Olympic Development team for three years in a row, this need not be restated in the essay. What could make a powerful essay would be a reflection about the pressure the student felt that third time around when everyone (except maybe the player himself) expected success. Depth rather than breadth should be the goal here.

- Biographical narratives: Some colleges specifically ask the applicant to write about a person who has had a major influence on the student's life. Constructing such essays can be tricky because it is easy to get caught up describing the other person and forget about—or run out of space for—writing about yourself. If you do choose to write about a grandparent or other mentor, be sure to explain how the relationship changed you. Some of the best student essays I've seen written about other people involve quirky characters met on bus stops or in diners. Distance from the characters seems to help.

- The epiphany: Often students are drawn to eye-opening, "ah-ha" moments as subjects for their college essays. While life-changing moments such as sports injuries, deaths in the family, or relocation can make for good writing, applicants need not feel that they must conclude from their epiphany that they are now completely mature, fully formed human beings. Colleges understand that high school students are works in progress. Young writers needn't be afraid of portraying themselves as occasionally confused and somewhat inexperienced. College admissions officers appreciate youthful optimism.

I also recommend that students stay away from volumes of "Best College Essays." Reading through these models may give a teenager a better idea of what is possible, but they can also be discouraging. I wish someone would come out with a collection of "So-So College Essays That Still Get the Job Done." Reading through these, students would say, "I could do that. You know something, I think I can do better than that."

Here are two sample college application essays by Patrick James that do the job quite nicely, demonstrating both narrative skill and authentic student voice.

College Essay

Soccer has been an important part of my life. From the competitive nature of the world to time management, the sport has taught me important lessons. It has been my mentor, teaching and molding me into the man I am.

Even as a child I loved the game. I enjoyed waking up Saturday mornings strapping on my shin guards, cleats, and other soccer gear and heading off to the fields. The smell of freshly cut grass brings me back to these days and puts a smile on my face. As I got older, the game became more serious to me. I started to care deeply about winning, and my competitive nature was unleashed. I quit the recreational league and did what any aspiring soccer player would do— joined a club team. In order to play on a competitive team and participate in the Olympic Development Program, I traveled an hour to practice several times a week and played games and tournaments on the weekends. Juggling a rigorous class load and soccer forced me to manage my time wisely. I would come home late every Tuesday and Thursday night and be faced with hours of homework. Somehow I found a balance between the two that allowed me to succeed in both. Now, when faced with unit tests or term projects, I am no longer daunted. I have the confidence in me to know that I can get the work done.

During a soccer game, there are twenty-two players on the field, eleven per side. Soccer isn't a sport of superstars, and every last player is needed to win the game. This aspect of the sport trained and crafted me into a natural team player. I have been a part of an alliance for so long on the field that I feel at home working with others off the field.

On every team there must be a leader, someone whom the players look up to and respect. On my high school team I was that leader. With the captain band worn proudly around my arm, I led our team to the quarterfinals of the CIF championships while breaking almost every record in Santa Monica High School soccer history. I led not by scoring goals, but from the backfield. Through years of club soccer and ODP I was able to acquire a knowledge for the game that most players do not have. I can read the game and see plays that are going to happen a few steps ahead of my teammates. With this experience I was able to help others look better and ultimately play to their potential. Forwards got the glory, but I had the satisfaction of knowing where the play began. Leadership is a quality that is not teachable, but instead instinctive. It is the aura that is given off by some people that makes others follow. Not only did soccer show me that I was a natural leader, but it also allowed me to develop this quality.

I had always assumed that I would go off to college and play Division One soccer. There was no doubt in my mind, it was as if it already happened and the case was closed. I received recruiting letters, and visited the colleges to speak to coaches and get a taste of campuses. I came home more inspired than ever to play Division One soccer. That is when I received the bad news. I had an MRI taken on my knee and the results were disastrous.

When I found out that I had torn my ACL, the most important stabilizing ligament in the knee, I did not know how to feel. I was devastated that I was going to have major reconstructive surgery and be off the field for at least six months, but I also felt a sense of liberation. I began to consider colleges for more than how good their team was and who the coach is. I came to the realization that soccer has served me well and taught me many important lessons, but that I did not necessarily need the sport to become who I wanted to be. It was at this point when I made the biggest decision in my life. I was going to hang up my Division One boots and leave the side of my mentor. It was time for me to get out on my own, see the world outside the box of soccer and go to a college where I could concentrate on my academic interests and plan for my career. The University of California offers me the chance to do just this. I plan to study history with an emphasis on economics. Having traveled through Europe and to Africa and Indonesia with my British father, I can imagine applying what I learn beyond the borders of this country. I hope—idealistic as this may sound—that I can use the lessons of history and apply them to help make ours a more peaceful and prosperous world.

Although it was hard to leave soccer as a boy, it was easy to become a man.

I Am a Camera

I am a camera. I open and close. I record. I try to see everything, but focus on what my lens captures. My film is truth, truth applied to images. Images don't escape me. I snap them and store them. I can develop them later—or not, as the camera chooses. As a camera, I function smoothly, but I am aware that all too often the camera has bias. Sometimes I become more than a camera when I recall data from memory and develop it. If I notice the slightest blemish on the developed image, then I am forced to interpret, to make judgements. My images are shaded by loyalties, I am loyal to the images I develop, conscious of the absolute value of those friendships. Those negatives I treasure, cosset in their sleeves. But I know that I could, perhaps, use my wide-angle lens a little more. Sometimes I turn the camera on myself—an expression of control, hasty, assertive, another imperfect image.

My true skill is with people, whether or not they see me, whether or not they suspect that the camera is me. I click quietly, using my many lenses, manipulating the view, foreshadowing the result. My subjects rarely hear the click; even if they do, how can they ever know that I am the camera, that the clicking comes from me, is me? Later in my dark room, I develop, interpret, embellish my images. I make time for my favorites, even allow them some control over the camera. Even so, the camera has power: image to negative; negative to positive; positive to truth. Only I know what I am doing. Only the camera understands.

The camera travels happily, visible but unseen. Wherever I go, the steady click-click accompanies me. Sometimes images develop their own presence, their own power. The camera gave the images life, and then they grew. The camera knows that, allows that. The camera moves relentlessly on, zooming in at will. It opens and closes until the job is done, wanting to produce the perfect images, for themselves and for the camera's own rewards.

The camera is direct, blunt, pulls no punches as it clicks, as it sees. I know how clearly it sees because the camera is me.

FOUR

Ω

Writing About Literature

In writing you work toward a result you won't see for years, and
can't be sure you'll ever see. It takes stamina and self-mastery and
faith. It demands those things of you, then gives them back with a
little extra, a surprise to keep you coming. It toughens you and
clears your head. I could feel it happening. I was saving my life
with every word I wrote, and I knew it.
　　　—Tobias Wolff, *In Pharoah's Army, Memoirs of the Lost War*

Assessment Instruments and Rubrics

Though writing about literature is not one of the NAEP writing types,
it is generally considered an important and lasting outcome of a high
school education. In California, students are asked to write a Response
to Literature at both the fourth- and the seventh-grade levels. The
California High School Exit Exam also includes what is called a Response to Literary/Expository Text. Students are asked to read a text—
short story, poem, or nonfiction passage—and to write an essay about
what they have read. In spring of 2001 seventh graders read the story
"To Sleep Under the Stars" by Carol Shaw Graham and were then
instructed to do the following:

Write an essay in which you present your understanding of the characters and the overall meaning of the story. Support your ideas with

examples and/or evidence from the text. Your writing will be evaluated on how well you write an essay that:

- shows your understanding of the author's message and your insight into the characters and ideas presented in the story;
- is organized around several clear ideas and/or images from the story; and
- justifies your interpretation by giving examples and citing evidence from the text.

As the California Standards Test Scoring Rubric indicates, students had to respond to both parts of the prompt, explaining both their understanding of characters and their understanding of the story in order to earn a score of 3 or 4. This same rubric is used to score all four writing types seventh graders may be asked to demonstrate: fictional or autobiographical narrative, response to literature, persuasion, summary. The rubric in Figure 4–1 explains the additional bullet points particular to each writing type, and indicates the corresponding scores.

It is important that teachers be familiar with the rubrics used to score their students' writing on state tests, but it is not vital that teachers should use the state's four-point scale in the classroom. In my experience, a six-point rubric offers much more specific information to young writers and parents. Of course scorers can whip through mountains of student papers more quickly and accurately using a four-point scale, but in the classroom rubrics serve different purposes. They are not measuring sticks but teaching tools.

Student Papers and Scoring Guides

At my high school we continue to employ a six-point department rubric even though the California High School Exit Exam rubric is a four-point scale. We feel the six-point rubric gives us more room to describe student improvement over the course of the year. Some of us would prefer a nine-point scale similar to the one the College Board uses to score Advanced Placement essays. Our Santa Monica High School English Department scoring guide reflects countless hours of

---

California Standards Test Scoring Rubric
Grade 7 Writing Tasks

4

The Writing
- clearly addresses all parts of the writing task
- demonstrates a clear understanding of purpose and audience
- maintains a consistent point of view, focus, and organizational structure, including the effective use of transitions
- includes a clearly presented central idea with relevant facts, details, and/or explanations
- includes a variety of sentence types
- contains few, if any, errors in the conventions of the English language (grammar, punctuation, capitalization, spelling). These errors do not interfere with the reader's understanding of the writing.

Fictional or Autobiographical Narrative
- provides a thoroughly developed plot line, including major and minor characters and a definite setting
- includes appropriate strategies (e.g., dialogue; suspense; narrative action)

Response to Literature
- develops interpretations that demonstrate a thoughtful, comprehensive grasp of the text
- organizes accurate and coherent interpretations around clear ideas, premises, or images from the literary work
- provides specific textual examples and details to support the interpretations

Persuasion
- authoritatively defends a position with precise and relevant evidence and convincingly addresses the reader's concerns, biases, and expectations

Summary
- is characterized by paraphrasing of the main idea(s) and significant details

---

FIGURE 4–1 *California standards test scoring rubric: grade 7 writing task*

3

The Writing
- clearly addresses all parts of the writing task
- demonstrates a general understanding of purpose and audience
- maintains a mostly consistent point of view, focus, and organizational structure, including the effective use of some transitions
- presents a central idea with mostly relevant facts, details, and explanations
- includes a variety of sentence types
- contains some errors in the conventions of the English language (grammar, punctuation, capitalization, spelling). These errors do not interfere with the reader's understanding of the writing.

Fictional or Autobiographical Narrative
- provides an adequately developed plot line, including major and minor characters and a definite setting
- includes appropriate strategies (e.g., dialogue; suspense; narrative action)

Response to Literature
- develops interpretations that demonstrate a comprehensive grasp of the text
- organizes accurate and reasonably coherent interpretations around clear ideas, premises, or images from the literary work
- provides textual examples and details to support the interpretations

Persuasion
- generally defends a position with relevant evidence and addresses the reader's concerns, biases, and expectations

Summary
- is characterized by paraphrasing of the main idea(s) and significant details

2

The Writing
- addresses only parts of the writing task
- demonstrates a little understanding of purpose and audience

FIGURE 4–1 *Continued*

- maintains an inconsistent point of view, focus, and organizational structure, which may include ineffective or awkward transitions that do not unify important ideas
- suggests a central idea with limited facts, details, and/or explanations
- includes little variety in sentence types
- contains several errors in the conventions of the English language (grammar, punctuation, capitalization, spelling). These errors may interfere with the reader's understanding of the writing.

Fictional or Autobiographical Narrative
- provides a minimally developed plot line, including characters and a setting
- attempts to use strategies but with minimal effectiveness (e.g., dialogue; suspense; narrative action)

Response to Literature
- develops interpretations that demonstrate a limited grasp of the text
- includes interpretations that lack accuracy or coherence as related to ideas, premises, or images from the literary work
- provides few, if any, textual examples and details to support the interpretations

Persuasion
- defends a position with little, if any, evidence and may address the reader's concerns, biases, and expectations

Summary
- is characterized by substantial copying of key phrases and minimal paraphrasing

1

The Writing
- addresses only one part of the writing task
- demonstrates no understanding of purpose and audience
- lacks a point of view, focus, organizational structure, and transitions that unify important ideas
- includes no sentence variety

FIGURE 4–1 *Continued*

- contains serious errors in the conventions of the English language (grammar, punctuation, capitalization, spelling). These errors interfere with the reader's understanding of the writing.

Fictional or Autobiographical Narrative
- lacks a developed plot line
- fails to use strategies (e.g., dialogue; suspense; narrative action)

Response to Literature
- demonstrates little grasp of the text
- lacks an interpretation or may be a simple retelling of the passage
- lacks textual examples and details

Persuasion
- fails to defend a position with any evidence and fails to address the reader's concerns, biases, and expectations

Summary
- is characterized by paraphrasing of indiscriminately selected phrases or sentences

FIGURE 4–1 *Continued*

negotiation among teachers and much borrowing from other rubrics, particularly the Subject A scoring guide used to assess the writing skills of incoming freshmen to the University of California. I have no doubt that our rubric will continue to evolve as we continue to find better ways to describe what we see and what we don't see in student papers.

In an ideal world, teachers would tweak this generic rubric for each assignment. The College Board does for this every AP writing prompt they use. You can find copies of these custom-written rubrics for the last few years' exams at <*http://www.collegeboard.org/ap/english /index.html*>. Alas, few teachers meeting 150 students every day have the time to create individualized scoring guides for each separate writing assignment.

Multiple Traits Scoring

Some schools and districts have begun using multiple traits scoring in place of holistic scoring. This approach allows for more description of the particular features of good writing. Student papers are evaluated separately for their ideas, organization, voice, word choice, sentence fluency, conventions, and presentation. The most powerful aspect of multiple trait scoring is the way it creates a common vocabulary for writing instruction. In Olathe Unified School District in Kansas, for example, teachers use the same language when talking about writing to students from grades 1 though 12. Common terminology can help demystify writing instruction both for students and for new teachers. More detailed information on multiple traits scoring is available on the Northwest Regional Laboratories website at *<http://www.nwrel.org/eval /writing/>*.

One English Department's Rubric

The Santa Monica High School rubric reflects our department's focus on analytical writing about literature. Each semester students are expected to write two analytical essays in response to a text and a third, personal or creative piece. Though we periodically reexamine our assumptions about literature-based writing as a standard, we keep coming back to it. One reason is that we are committed to ensuring that the door to Advanced Placement classes in the eleventh and twelfth grades remains open to all students. If such analytic writing is taught only in ninth- and tenth-grade honors classes—with other students writing personal essays and creative stories—only honors students will be prepared for AP coursework. A powerful argument can be made, of course, (and often is at spirited department meetings) that we are overlooking the needs of students who have no intention or desire to take advanced placement classes. Are these students being shortchanged by a curriculum that values analysis over creative expression?

We will probably struggle with this issue for a long time to come. There is no easy answer. In the meantime we have agreed on a department writing assessment that asks students to read a short story or passage and then write an essay in response. Together we assess student papers holistically using the scoring guide in Figure 4–2.

Last year we used an excerpt from Richard Rodriguez's from *Hunger of Memory*, which had once appeared on the AP Language exam, for

Santa Monica High School English Department Analytical Essay Scoring Guide, Grades 9–12

A **6** paper presents an insightful analysis of the text, elaborating with well-chosen examples and persuasive reasoning. It has mature development and style. The 6 paper shows that its writer can use a variety of sophisticated sentences effectively, observe the conventions of written English, and choose words aptly.

A **5** paper presents a thoughtful and well-organized analysis of the text, elaborating with appropriate examples and sensible reasoning. It may contain minor errors of fact or interpretation. A 5 paper typically has a less fluent and complex style than a 6, but does show that its writer can vary sentences effectively, observe the conventions of written English, and usually choose words aptly.

A **4** paper presents an adequate analysis of the text, elaborating with sufficient examples and acceptable reasoning. It may contain some errors of fact or interpretation. Just as these examples and this reasoning will ordinarily be less developed than those in 5 papers, so will the 4 paper's style be less effective. Nevertheless, a 4 paper shows that its writer can usually control sentences of reasonable variety, observe the conventions of written English, and choose words of sufficient precision.

A **3** paper demonstrates some understanding of the text and prompt, but relevant analysis is minimal or absent. It may substantially misread or oversimplify the text. The paper may rely on plot summary, inappropriate or insufficient evidence, or move directly from evidence to inference. Its prose is usually characterized by at least one of the following: frequently imprecise word choice; little sentence variety; occasional major errors in grammar and usage, or frequent minor errors.

A **2** paper has serious weaknesses, ordinarily of several kinds. It frequently presents a simplistic or incoherent response, one that may suggest a major misunderstanding of the text or the prompt. It lacks specific evidence. Its prose is usually characterized by at least one of the following: simplistic or inaccurate word choice; monotonous or fragmented sentence structure; many repeated errors in grammar and usage.

A **1** paper suggests severe difficulties in reading and writing conventional English. It may disregard the prompt's demands, or it may lack any appropriate pattern of structure or development. It may be inappropriately brief. It often has a pervasive pattern of errors in word choice, sentence structure, grammar, and usage.

FIGURE 4–2 *Santa Monica high school English department analytical essay scoring guide, grades 9–12*

our tenth- and eleventh-grade, departmentwide writing assessment. Students had two class periods to complete the task: one day for reading and marking the text, the next for writing. Students were not allowed to meet in groups to talk about the passage nor were teachers allowed to discuss it with the class. On the second day we handed students the prompt that we had simplified from the original AP version:

Directions for Writing

You have read and marked up a passage written by Richard Rodriguez, whose parents immigrated from Mexico and raised their family in California. Analyze the relationships among various family members. Use specific evidence from the story to support your thesis.

The following student paper was scored a 4, just below the level required by the department to enroll in AP honors English. I would have scored the paper higher, probably on the basis of the Icarus allusion and "tiny granny eyes" expression alone. To me, such things suggest a student who enjoys taking chances both with interpretation and with writing. This brings up an issue I often struggle with when reading essays against a rubric. Yes, a scoring guide helps minimize idiosyncratic responses. We have had many fewer student complaints about grades since all members of the department began using the same scoring guide. At the same time, some papers simply don't fit into any category neatly. These unclassifiable pieces of writing squirm about in my hands, unscored, until I sometimes give up and slap an "A" on the paper for originality. It is one thing to try to assure consistency in a state- or districtwide scoring session. It's quite another to attempt to "norm" teachers as readers of student papers forever. I hope I never become perfectly "normed."

Blue Paradise

In the passage we were given to read we see the world through the eyes of one of the children in this family. He tells a story of how his family went from poor to rich. Without knowing it he is telling the story of a family Icarus who flew too high to the sun, only to plummet into a world where money is everything leaving no room for love. The family that we see from the start was very poor, in the way that she says: "Someday . . . you will all grow up and all be very rich." I know from this quote that she must have been brought up, lived, and brought her children up in a destitute home environment. Because money is the one thing she herself can't have she assumes—like many do—that it is the answer to all her life's problems.

Christmas comes again one year when the children have all grown up and become prestigious and wealthy. The son remarks: "Her feet are wreathed with gifts . . . she seems so sad to me . . . sad that it was not quite, can never be, the Christmas Her son recalls past Christmas' when he sees the sadness in his mother's eyes. He assumes she is unhappy, even though this year as she had previously wished she had tons of precious gifts. She's got a fur coat so thick it covers her tiny granny eyes as if preventing her from seeing her mistake in trading family togetherness for money.

As the children are leaving and the son is putting a coat on his father, the son discovers something about the night: "It is, I realize, the only thing that he has said to me all evening." Again we see the gap, the rift so great the son doesn't even realize his father hasn't spoken to him once on Christmas.

This story seems familiar to me because on my mother's side it happened in her own family. My grandma sits alone at home while her kids go off and make a ¾ billion. All except my mom . . . and I'm happy for that. Money sometimes may seem like an answer, but be careful what you wish for, you just might get it. As the son remarked to his mother: "Such are the questions of paradise, mama."

By Eva McDaniel

The two teachers who read this essay felt that Eva was not specific enough in her analysis of the relationships among the various family members. To give you an idea what they were looking for, here is an essay on the same assessment that was scored a 5. As happens in many holistic scoring sessions, only a handful of the tenth- and eleventh-grade papers among the 1,150 were scored with a 6. Remember as you read that this is a first draft.

Emotional Isolation

The Rodriquez family has gone through dramatic changes spanning only one generation: the change from lower to upper class and the change from emotional closeness to cold, distant relationships. These two changes are inextricably intertwined: perhaps financial security and independence issolate each family member because the need for each others' support is no longer apparent. Whatever the causes the Rodriquezs' are now estranged and emotionally isolated.

Mrs. Rodriguez predicted that, as adults, they would not have emotional bonds. As children she used to tell them how rich and succesful they would be as adults. "But," she warned them, "you'll only be able to see my eyes." The eyes symbolize that this is the level of depth that they will have in their relationships. Their relationships do not span over their hearts, faces, and arms. The limited use of body parts represents the limits their relationships will have. Mrs. Rodriguez's prediction has come true.

However even though they can see each other's eyes, the sheer lack of completeness in their relationships make even the most trivial bond a struggle. The world her children live in is a mystery to Mrs. Rodriguez. As the children leave she is described, "looking into the dark where expensive foreign cars idle sharply." This is symbolic of Mrs. Rodriguez's relationship with her children. Richard Rodriguez's diction here reveals the issolation Mrs. Rodriguez feels: "looking into the dark" suggests that, when observing her children's lives, she is completely lost. In the dark one can't see. Mrs. Rodriguez can't decipher or understand her children and their luxurious lifestyles. Richard Rodriguez describes their vehicles as "foreign" and "sharp." The cars represent the children and how, emotionaly, they are completely foreign, estranged, and uncomforting to their mother. Their success seperates them from their parents, making close relationships a challenge none of them are willing to take on.

Mr. Rodriguez is the least willing to rebuild relationships because he doesn't make any effort to reach out to his children. Upon leaving Mr. Rodriquez asks Richard if he is going home now. Richard realizes "it is … the only thing that he ha said to me all evening." While the rest of the family goes through the actions, empty as they may be, of pretending to be a family, Mr. Rodriguez humors no one:

his disappointement in his chidren is evident by the fact that he doesn't even try to get to know them anymore. To him, they are too far gone to reach out to.

The Rodriguez family's lack of an emotional connection is evident in that, symbolicly, children can only see their parents' eyes, not their hearts. Also, the childrens' financial success and independence has made them different from their parents and therefore unable to relate to eachother, and some of them don't even try to feel or create a substantial bond because they are already so issolated from eachother. These circumstances are partly caused by the change of social class the family has undergone. Every change a family goes through has it's benefits and drawbacks—hopefully other families will keep appreciating and loving eachother even after they go their separate ways.

By Ellen Eggebroten

I think it is easy to see that for both Eva and Ellen writing about literature is a challenging yet appropriate task. They clearly understand the Rodriguez passage and know how to construct a defensible analysis of the text. It is not so easy to make the case for literary analysis with other students. In the next essay the writer, Paloma, seems overwhelmed, almost frightened, by what she has been asked to do. Her essay was written in response to the department's ninth-grade prompt. The same rules applied. Students had two class periods for reading and writing and were not allowed to discuss the story among themselves.

Writing Directions

You have read the short story "If the River Was Whiskey" by T. C. Boyle. Think about the ways Tiller feels and acts when he is with his father or when he thinks about him. Also think about the ways Tiller's father feels and acts when he's with Tiller or thinks about him.

Write an essay analyzing the relationship between Tiller and his father.

- In your first paragraph, include a thesis statement that tells your main idea about their relationship.

- As you write your essay, support your ideas with reasons and evidence from the story.

Paloma's paper was scored a 2 for its lack of development and lack of concrete detail. Though scorers are not meant to comment on the student papers, the word "Vague!" was scribbled across the first page. The essay was also criticized for using only two paragraphs. It seems to me that the student set out with good intentions and a relatively clear idea about how to approach this writing task but then simply ran out of steam. Maybe Paloma gave up because she hadn't learned how to approach an essay in the way Anne Lamotte's father advised his son, "bird by bird." The student clearly seems to have the reading skills and mechanical skills she needs to complete the assignment. Something else is causing her to stall as a writer.

Untitled

In the short story "If the River Was Whiskey" by T. C. Boyle, a boy and his father's relationship is portrayed. Tiller, the boy, is completely in denial about his father's problems. His father thinks of Tiller as something he can not control, since he has so many problems himself. There relationship is obvious when certain sitiations occur.

The scene in the boat with tiller and his father is sybolical to Tiller's perception of his father. When the two are out on the lake hoping to catch a pike, Tiller's father feels a pull at the rod. The two excitingly try to reel it back in, hoping to find a pike. But it turns out to be just a carp. "With his beard and long hair and with the crumpled suffering look on his face, he was the picture of the crucified Christ Tiller had contemplated a hundred times at church . . . This was no pike. It was a carp. A fat, pouty, stinking, ugly mud carp. Trash fish . . . Tiller looked at his father and felt like crying." Tiller's expectations of his father to catch a pike were very high, and when Tiller realizes it is not a pike, he doesn't have the heart to tell his father. This scene shows that Tiller is in denial about all the negative things about his father. He sees his father as a Christ-like figure, but deep down inside he knows that that is not true, and that makes him very sad.

by Paloma Montoya

Having a department assessment in place and then preserving these student performances in their portfolios has had a powerful effect upon the teaching of writing in the English department. The scoring sessions help us to be consistent and offer multiple opportunities for working through differences of opinion. The sessions also help new teachers feel more confident in their grading.

When Paloma came to me the following year in tenth grade, I was able to read her ninth-grade paper and see immediately that here was an insightful reader who hadn't developed the confidence to write an extended essay about literature. I wish I could say that I did x, y, and z and voilà, an accomplished writer emerged. In fact, Paloma continued to struggle throughout the year, often not turning in essays rather than submitting something she felt was shabby. Talking with her ninth-grade teacher, I discovered that this had been her pattern the year before. In a parent conference with the student present, Paloma's mother told me how Paloma would sit for hours in her room, trying to work on her writing assignments but making little or no progress.

Scaffolding for Struggling Writers

Helping students move from paralysis to product is a huge challenge for writing teachers. Many students look at papers like Ellen's and wonder how she saw all of this in the short Rodriguez passage. My job is to help students see for themselves how lines in a text can be deconstructed for meaning. One graphic organizer I call a Reflection chart (Figure 4–3) often helps students like Paloma gather ideas about what they have read.

I handed this chart out to students when we neared the end of Maxine Hong Kingston's *The Woman Warrior*. I knew that students would soon have to write an essay on the book (they probably did as well, but teenagers have a special talent for blocking out bad news). Rather than terrify students like Paloma with a writing prompt, essay guidelines, and due dates, I asked the class to choose several quotations from the final section of the book that interested them and use

Reflection Chart

Quote from the chapter (include page number)	What I think	What this says about the book	What this says about the world

FIGURE 4–3 *Reflection chart*

the Reflection chart to help them think about the significance of these passages. Paloma wrote:

Quote from the chapter
"Maybe because I was the one with the tongue cut loose, I had grown inside me a list of over two hundred things that I had to tell my mother so that she would know the true things about me and stop the pain in my throat." Page 197

What I think
In this quote Maxine Hong Kingston shows her thoughts and regrets during the period when she was living at home with her parents.

What this says about the book
This quote shows that MHK didn't feel comfortable enough to discuss everything about her life with her mother when she was young so instead she bottled up all of the emotions insider her and she is ready to burst. She needs a cure.

What this says about the world
MHK is not the only person who hides things from her mother. The fact that she thinks by telling her mom her secrets will make her feel better shows that she needs her mom for comfort. She feels bad about hiding things from her. I think this goes for everyone who has ever hidden something from their parents.

Not only did students find this a relatively painless task, but the results provided them with excellent material for writing a cohesive essay. Filling out the chart helps students begin to see how passages can be analyzed on several different levels. It pushes them past their own first impressions to genuine literary analysis. How many times have you written on student papers "So? What is the significance of this quotation?" This exercise trains students to explore the significance of a quote step by step. Sepehr, a young man who has been in this country for only four years and is himself living between two cultural worlds, wrote:

Quote from the chapter
"I thought every house had to have its crazy woman or crazy girl, every village its idiot. Who would be it at our house? Probably me."

What I think
The constant criticism of her clumsiness and faults has degraded her self-esteem into nothing.
What this says about the book
The book shows how these foolish customs can cause such deep wounds in one's character which will leave its scars forever.
What this says about the world
We must do all we can to stop the customs that induce so much unnecessary pain and destruction of lives.

After students have worked on their charts for about thirty minutes, I ask them to share their work with a partner. Often this develops into rich conversations about the book with the two readers exploring even more deeply the significance of their quotations. Five minutes before the end of class I have every student read aloud one entry from the last column. It is always amazing to hear how much the various passages have in common. Moving from these observations of what various quotations say about the world to a thesis statement for an essay on *The Woman Warrior* suddenly seems doable.

Five Things to Do with a Quotation

Inexpert writers, writing about literature, have somehow acquired the notion that preparing to write an essay means going on a "quotations" hunt. Again and again students thumb through their books looking for "good quotes" before they have a clear idea of what it is they want to write. They pepper their papers with these quotations and then wonder how I can say that their thesis is unsupported. A master teacher and colleague of mine at Santa Monica High School, Meredith Louria, created the following worksheet to help students learn how to use quotations effectively.

Five Things to Do with a Quotation

1. Analyze a word and/or image from the quote. Explain how the word's denotation and connotation reveal or reinforce the meaning of the passage. Explain how the image's sensory details reveal or reinforce the point the quote illustrates.

Example

Nick looks back on Gatsby's life and says, "it is what preyed on Gatsby, what foul dust floated in the wake of his dreams" (Fitzgerald 6). The use of the word "preyed" gives the idea that Gatsby is under attack. The shift to sympathetic diction shows the change in tone towards the American Dream. The Dreamer is no longer one who prospers; the word "prey" implies helplessness and the eventual loss of a battle. Gatsby is symolically being hunted by his own aspirations, which stem from the idea of the American Dream. The "dust" that surrounds Gatsby prevents him from being seen for what he really is. Dust clouds, but does not completely obscure, what it surrounds. Because of this, Gatsby's life seems glorious but in reality Gatsby is no more than a victim. (Jackie Len)

2. Explain how the information in the quote relates to a significant action, characterization, or idea from the text. You are pointing out an important connection the reader might not have noticed.

Example

In an attempt to impress the woman he loves, Gatsby uses his wealth and expensive belongings to influence her impression of him. "He took out a pile of shirts and began throwing them one by one before us, shirts of sheer linen and thick silk and fine flannel . . . Suddenly with a strained sound Daisy bent her head into the shirts and began to cry stormily . . . "It makes me sad because I've never seen such—such beautiful shirts before" (Fitzgerald 97–98). Gatsby's tactics prove successful in impressing Daisy. Daisy's crying is evidence that she is deeply touched by mere possessions. The beauty that she sees in a pile of shirts is enough to bring her to tears, which shows the deeply embedded values she places on wealth and its appearance. (Aaron Sherman)

3. Sometimes what a quote *doesn't* say is more important than its surface details. Explain how the information the quote *lacks* relates to a significant action, characterization, or idea from the text.

Example

Willy says, "at the age of eighty-four, he made his living . . . when he died—and by the way he died the death of a salesman, in his green velvet slippers in the smoker of the New York, New Haven and Hartford, going to Boston—when he died, hundreds of salesmen and buyers were at his funeral" (Miller 81). Willy aspires to be like Dave Singleman and fails to see the negative parts of Singleman's life. He works up till the day he dies, when he dies on the job. No family or friends attend his funeral, only business acquaintances. (Katie Ryan)

4. Discuss the symbolism of an object mentioned in the quotation.

Example

In describing Gatsby's obsession with Daisy, Nick says "he had committed himself to the following of a grail" (Fitzgerald 156). According to medieval times, the grail is a magic cup which people who are not meant to drink out of, and do, die. Like the grail, Daisy is magic in Gatsby's eyes. Gatsby has everything people think the "American Dream" means; however, much like the followers of the grail, Gatsby desperately searches for Daisy to make him feel complete. Much like the followers of the grail, Gatsby ends up dying indirectly trying to attain the magic he needed to fill the emotional void in his life. (Nancy Argueta)

5. Explain the irony of the quotation. Discuss both the literal level of the quotation, and its ironic implications.

Example

Gatsby's funeral is a great disappointment. "The minister glanced several times at his watch so I took him aside and asked him to wait for half an hour. But it wasn't any use. Nobody came" (Fitzgerald 182). During the novel Gatsby would throw huge, lavish parties with tons of people there. The irony is that not one of those people showed up at his funeral. While accomplishing the American Dream, Gatsby had no time to make friends. The parties he threw were just his way of playing the part of someone who has achieved the American Dream. He forfeited having close relationships to reach his dream of being rich and powerful. (Yvette Vasquez)

One more "thing to do with a quotation" that I have found effective is to ask students to consider how other, more common or obvious word choices would alter the meaning of the line.

Culminating Assignments That Don't Feel Like Hard Work

Learning to write about literature is an important and lasting outcome of a high school education. Making this somewhat specialized type of writing authentic for students, particularly for reluctant scholars, keeps me ever on the lookout for assignments that engage them in unexpected ways. My teaching objective for each of the following writing tasks is to have students reflect on what they have read and written over the course of the year, make new connections, and develop new insights. The following assignments work best when students have a list in front of them of all the books they have read in a given school year. I have students keep a reading log in their portfolios.

- Ask students to imagine that two characters from the books they have read this semester just sat down next to one another at a Santa Monica bus stop. What would they say to one another? (I've received some wonderful dialogues between Holden Caulfield and Richard Wright, the hunchback of Notre Dame and Grendel, Victor Frankenstein and Dr. Jekyll.)
- Have students read Wallace Steven's "Thirteen Ways of Looking at a Blackbird" and then write a poem of their own entitled "Thirteen Ways of Looking at Odysseus, or Juliet, or Huck Finn, or Jack from *Lord of the Flies*."
- Students choose an ordinary subject (soup, the wind, feet) and write about it in the style of the authors they have read; for example, in an American Literature class: Poe, Hawthorne, Hemingway, Dickinson, Whitman, and Ginsberg.
- Of all the fictional worlds students entered in the course of a year's reading, ask them to choose the one they would most and least like to inhabit and to explain why.
- Of all the fictional characters students have come to know over the course of a year's reading, ask them to choose the one charac-

ter they would most and least like to know better and to explain why. As a variation you might ask students to identify the characters they would most and least like to wed.

- Have students imagine that they are movie studio executives. Ask them which of the books they read this year would be best suited for the big screen, which would never work, and why.
- Choose a book that might make a good "major motion picture." Have students imagine they are casting directors and cast the film with contemporary actors and actresses. Each choice must be explained.
- Have students write a letter to the English department chairperson recommending a title that should either be added or omitted from next year's curriculum.
- Have students write a letter to a student who will be in this class next year explaining what to expect—both good and bad. I have students sign their letters and then put them in sealed envelopes. I promise that the letters will remained sealed until opened by students on the first day of class the following year.

Are such writing assignments authentic responses to literature? I think so. Though they can be much more difficult to grade than a traditional essay, students can help by determining what they think would make an "A" response to one of these creative assignments. You don't need to generate a whole rubric, but simply identify qualities that an excellent paper embodies.

As Tobias Wolff explained, writing "toughens you and clears your head." Whether my students are crafting traditional essays or imitating "The Raven," I believe they are saving their lives with every word they write.

FIVE

Ω

Cohesive Writing—The Product

One of the greatest obstacles to cohesive student writing is the lack of clear thinking. It is not that kids don't know how to think or how to write, but rather they don't see the two things as intimately connected. They approach the act of writing as though it were a matter of transcribing from their brain to the page. James Joyce, Stephen King, and Joyce Carol Oates are the only writers I know who can work this way, but most thirteen-year-olds think that they should be able to churn out an essay or book report without troubling their brains. When nothing flows from the pen or their fingers seem paralyzed on the keyboard, they claim "writer's block" or simply give up, convinced they can't write.

The Writing Process Revisited

Students don't realize that writing is a powerful tool for figuring out what you think. They need to invest a good forty minutes scribbling down their thoughts for an essay without concern for organization or even thesis development. How can you know what it is you want to prove until you play with the ideas a bit? I can't tell you how many student papers I have read whose writers discovered the thesis only in the final paragraph. This is natural. Unfortunately students often hand in these jottings as a finished essay.

Teachers do a disservice to students if they accept first-draft jottings as finished papers. Practice makes permanent, not perfect. Young writers who generate quantities of rough prose rife with errors and who are seldom made to revise and edit soon find that their mistakes have become ingrained. Students don't become better writers simply by writing a lot. They improve by writing *well* often. Requiring them to polish sentences that only vaguely express inchoate thoughts improves not only the writing but also their ideas and thinking processes. Hugh Blair, a preeminent nineteenth-century rhetorician whose lessons for writing influenced Abraham Lincoln, explained that:

> We may rest assured that, whenever we express ourselves ill, there is, besides the mismanagement of language, for the most part some mistake in our manner of conceiving the subject. Embarrassed, obscure, and feeble sentences are generally, if not always, the result of embarrassed, obscure, and feeble thought. Thought and language act and react upon each other mutually. Logic and rhetoric have here, as in many other cases, a strict connection; and he that is learning to arrange his sentences with accuracy and order is learning, at the same time, to think with accuracy and order. ([1783] 1965, 245–246)

One has only to think of Lincoln's Gettysburg Address to recognize the power of artfully chosen words in the service of important ideas. The country heard Lincoln's plain, short speech and was never quite the same. "Fourscore and seven years ago, our fathers brought forth upon this continent a new nation, conceived in liberty, and dedicated to the proposition that all men are created equal." Lincoln's "plain" language was far from artless. He had chosen his words and crafted his thoughts with accuracy and order.

To help students improve their feeble sentences, we are going to have to wean them from feeble thinking. This will require enormous effort. Popular culture bombards kids with seductive messages about how to think, how to dress, how to have fun, and how to be cool. "Chilling," not rigorous thinking, is the mental state of choice.

The Gettysburg Address represents a lifetime of robust thinking about whether a nation conceived in liberty and dedicated to the proposition that all men are created equal "can long endure." Lincoln believed it could and in 272 words convinced America.

Creating a classroom where clear thinking and clear writing thrive is no simple matter. The first part of this book examined guidelines for the kinds of cohesive writing students should be practicing in middle and high school. Now we must ask, how do these guidelines translate into practice? What does an effective writing program look like?

I don't believe there is any one perfect model or single, step-by-step process that teaches all students how to write well, guaranteed. What works with one group of students sometimes fails with the next. What I am inspired to teach in the fall may bore me silly in the spring. I know this sounds messy. Sometimes it is. The following set of beliefs keep me focused.

1. In order to learn to write, one must write.
2. Authentic tasks and topics generate the most cohesive student writing.
3. Students need both supportive and critical feedback.
4. There is no cohesive writing without revision.

Learning to Write by Writing

If students are to become accomplished, effective writers, they are going to have to generate a lot of writing. Of course it is one thing for a professor at the University of Iowa Writers' Workshop to tell this to twelve graduate students and quite another for me to say the same to my 150 charges, every one of them under age eighteen. Somehow I need to find ways for students to generate many more pages of writing than I am ever going to be able to read. I am convinced that young writers who receive regular, one-on-one attention from teachers make more progress than those who don't. As things stand, however, there simply is not enough of me to go around.

I have made my peace with this situation by having students do a lot of writing that gets recorded but that I don't read with an evaluative eye. These in-class assignments are designed to help students better understand something we have read or to lay the groundwork for class discussion, but along with serving this instructional purpose, I find that they also build students' writing skills. Students need to develop the habit of crafting sentences and finding words to match their thoughts. Just as an athlete develops muscles and practices moves until they are almost automatic, so novice writers need to build stamina and fluency. How can we expect students to perform well on a high-stakes writing assignment without giving them multiple opportunities to practice on low-stakes tasks? Putting pen to paper for five to ten minutes a day is a profitable practice.

Peter Elbow (2000) makes an excellent case for such low-stakes writing:

> Low-stakes writing helps students involve themselves in the ideas or subject matter of a course. It helps them find their own language for the issues of the course; they stumble into their own analogies and metaphors for academic concepts. Theorists are fond of saying that learning a discipline means learning its discourse, but learning a discipline also means learning *not* to use that discourse. That is, students don't know a field until they can write and talk about what's in the textbook and the lectures in their *own* lingo, in their informal, "home," or "personal" language—language that, as Vygotsky says, is "saturated with sense" or experience. (353)

Young writers need opportunities to practice expressing their feelings without fear that the grammar police will collar them or that they have to make perfect sense. I constantly remind students that they are not writing to demonstrate what they know but rather to discover what they think.

In California's standards-based curriculum there is little time for personal journal writing unconnected to the lesson at hand. Of course the topics I put to students often ask for a personal response to an idea or theme, but we aren't keeping diaries. For example, in preparation for discussing Daniel Keyes' story "Flowers for Algernon," I ask students to write for ten minutes and try to define the word "intelligence." Before handing out copies of *Julius Caesar*, I ask students to write about a time when they felt betrayed by a friend. After studying the poetry of Allen Ginsberg, students write their own, personal "Howl." Though students sometimes volunteer to read what they have written—they love sharing their Howls—most often they simply tell about what they have written. The writing helps students figure out what they think or make a personal connection.

It is important to collect all of these pieces or to have students date and save them in a notebook that is later collected. Otherwise, many students stop taking such writing seriously. A simple accountability system also rewards students who have been diligent with their writing. I take a cursory look at these papers and put a stamp or some other cryptic mark at the top of the page to indicate that I am cognizant the student did the work. Would it be better if I responded to these student quickwrites? Of course; research has demonstrated the powerful effects of teacher/student dialogue journals. If I had time to carefully read these pieces of writing, I would know more clearly how well individual students comprehended the literature we were reading or the particular lesson at hand. Unfortunately, under the circumstances in which I work, I need to save my reading time for student drafts.

A few "writing-to-learn" sets of papers that I do read carefully, though only for their content, are page-long pieces asking students to give the gist of the last night's homework reading or to tell about the progress they are making in a particular book. I use these papers as a way of checking up on their reading. I tell them not to bother with fairy stories. If they haven't done the homework, just 'fess up and write about how they plan to catch up between now and tomorrow. The short papers on how the reading of *The Odyssey* or Mary Shelley's *Frankenstein* is progressing are important windows for me. I usually ask students to write these in class within the first few days of studying the text. I need to find out which students are foundering before they are lost forever to Cliff's Notes. I ask students to be very specific about what they are struggling with, not only to help me prescribe solutions but also to help students identify for themselves why this particular text is giving them trouble. Students don't need grades on these papers, They need help.

A Five-Day Writing Plan

Any high-stakes writing assignment must be clearly and carefully planned for students—not for the purpose of ensuring uniform products but rather to provide a structure upon which students' individual responses can grow. Figure 5–1 offers a snapshot of how I structure a unit in cohesive writing.

To illustrate this five-day plan, I will use a comparison/contrast writing assignment. For this particular lesson students need to begin their reading about a month before Day One. I tell students that they are going to read a book and watch a film, then write an essay comparing the two. Students usually become very excited at this prospect and bubble over with ideas of films based on books. While I am open to their suggestions (some of the best-ever pairings have come from students), I explain that we are looking for more in the comparison than simply a book made into a movie. The most interesting comparisons to explore are those where the filmmaker has a unique interpretation of the book's main idea or where a book and a film deal with similar themes in fundamentally different ways. I offer the following list of pairings that have worked well in the past and urge students to work with at least one other student so they will have someone with whom to talk about the book and view the film.

- *Emma* by Jane Austen and *Clueless*
- *The Hot Zone* by Richard Preston and *Outbreak*
- *Being There* by Jerzy Kozinski and *Forest Gump*
- *Do Androids Dream of Electric Sheep?* by Philip K. Dick and *Bladerunner*
- *One Flew over the Cuckoo's Nest* by Ken Kesey and the film of the same name

I warn these tenth-grade students that if any of the films they want to watch are rated R, they are going to need their parents' permission before I will OK the selection.

On Day One, I teach students about the two ways of organizing comparison/contrast papers: the point and block methods (Figure 5–2).

Day One	
Teacher:	Introduce assignment, guidelines, due dates, rubric
Students:	Discuss the topic, ask questions, explore ideas
	Homework: Draft a thesis statement
Day Two	
Teacher:	Check individual thesis statements
Students:	Collect supporting evidence from text, from friends, from the Internet, from the library
	Homework: Revise thesis, organize evidence in preparation for tomorrow's in-class essay
Day Three	
Teacher:	Maintain an environment for in-class writing. Collect papers at the end of the period.
Students:	Write an in-class essay
Day Four	
Teacher:	Offer lesson on recurring mechanical errors. Create peer editing groups based upon essay topics and/or student needs. Review guidelines for the format of a final draft.
Students:	Offer support and criticism on peers' drafts
	Homework: Revise!
Day Five	
Teacher:	Collect final drafts. Keep a record of student comments on the assignment.
Students:	Discuss final products. What would students do differently next time?

FIGURE 5–1 *A five-day writing plan*

Both include an introduction with titles, authors, and a clear thesis statement that sets out the comparison. The difference lies in the organization of the supporting paragraphs. Using the block method, a writer first talks about the book (or film) in terms of various criteria

Block Method	Point Method
Introduction	Introduction
Book • characters • tone, mood • author's purpose	Characters • book • film
	Tone, mood • book • film
Film • characters • tone, mood • filmmaker's purpose	Purpose • book • film
Conclusion	Conclusion

FIGURE 5–2 *Point and block methods compared*

(e.g., characters, tone, purpose) and then about the film (or book). In the point method supporting paragraphs focus on the criteria and then include a discussion of the book and film for each.

One of the trickiest aspects of this lesson is explaining it in such a way that students don't simply incorporate the examples I use for criteria of comparison into their essays. Following the explanation I put students into groups according to the book and film they have chosen and let them discuss what they have read and seen. After about twenty minutes I ask them to begin thinking about possible thesis statements for their essays. What is it about these two works that would be interesting to compare and contrast? For homework, they draft a working thesis.

On Day Two students return to their groups. While I circulate about the room checking thesis statements, making suggestions, and helping those who are stuck, students work together to find supporting evidence for their various thesis statements. This task inevitably draws them into deeper conversations about the book and film. Many decide to discard their first thesis for something more interesting and often more precise. One question that always comes up with the assignment is how to gather quotes from a movie. I simply tell students that quotations aren't the only way to support a thesis and to do the best they can when paraphrasing or using examples. Toward the end of the period we review the point and block methods of organization, and I urge students to decide which they plan to employ before they arrive to write tomorrow's in-class essay. Their homework is to make sure that they are satisfied with their thesis and that they have enough evidence at hand to support it. They should enter class tomorrow ready to write.

Day Three can be problematic. If students see this as free writing time for drafting an essay, many fritter away the hour and produce nothing that even resembles a draft. Some will tell you that they can't write in school. Others will say they don't know how to start and keep you talking at their desk, keeping other students from concentrating. On the other hand, if you make this first draft a homework assignment far too many (at least at my school in any but honors classes) arrive with little more than a few random notes. There is nothing for a peer to comment on. The next day's lesson is ruined. I try to make students feel that what we are doing on Day Three is a timed-writing task that they must complete before the end of the period. I don't do this because I feel writing under pressure builds character, but because it's one of the only ways I have found to make my reluctant writers produce. For that reason I collect the papers at the bell and prepare for a long night of reading.

Depending upon your own personal schedule or the number of papers you collect from students on Day Three, Day Four of this writing plan may not be the next day of the week. I find that I usually can read one class set of student papers overnight, but I am a fast reader. I believe that comments I make on these first drafts are much more valuable than any that appear on final copies. These are the essays that students are still going to work on. Why not tell them what I think now rather than later?

Arturo's comparison/contrast paper (below) clearly needs much work, but you can see that this is a young man with a lot of ideas. It is possible that my comments will seem overwhelming or even a bit chiding, but they were written in the spring, after we had been together as teacher and student for many months. Arturo knew I believed in him as a writer and that even my harsh comments were lovingly offered.

Though my comments on most students' drafts were written by hand in ink, I was able to respond to Arturo's typed draft in italics within his own text. There are eight computers in my classroom, and I encourage the first students who arrive to take up a writing station there. Our whole school is Internet-connected so students can email me the drafts from where they sit. I used to employ all capital letters when responding within a student paper, but I was stopped because it looked as though I was shouting at them on the page. Instead, I use boldface and italic type for my response.

First Draft
Block Method
Let Books be Books

In a book, the imagination is left to make a personal vivid picture of what a reader would see. ***I am finding your first sentence hard to follow, Arturo.*** All the hard work ***Why this reference to hard work?*** that goes into a movie will never capture the same feeling and overall sense of a book. *The Hot Zone* by Richard Preston and the movie *Outbreak* show that the final execution of a final product ***I'm lost. What execution?*** has its own limitation, whether it is a book or a movie.

Information wise, ***This is a hideous expression.*** content in a movie or book has to be appropriate in order to leave a lasting impression. ***Too vague. What are you trying to say here?*** In the format of a book, *The Hot Zone* is filled with so much information that can only take the format of a book. The definition of a virus was crucial to the book. ***Why was the "definition" crucial?*** that no information could be left out without leaving a void. "A virus is a small capsule make of membranes and proteins . . . Some biologists classify viruses as 'life forms . . .' The faucet (virus) runs and runs until the cell is exhausted, consumed, and destroyed" (p. 83–84). ***I think I have mentioned once or twice before that you don't need this p. for*** *page numbers* . . . The presentation of the material would initially interest a hard core science fiction reader, **Why?** but it is also done in a way that it does what it is supposed to accomplish. Absolute terror. **This sentence fragment is really effective.** The scene inside of USAMRIID in the movie *Outbreak* did a good job. **Weak expression "good job"** of showing the viewer how viruses and bacteria's are separated into biosafety levels 1 (in real life, biosaftey level 0), 2, 3, and 4. **For the purpose of this essay, why is it important to make this distinction?** The mysterious Motava virus sits in level 4 along with Ebola and Marburg. The new mysterious virus works very similar like Ebola. Entering the biosafety level 4 lab Dennis Hoffman and Kevin Spacey meet with Cuba Gooding Jr., **I'm not sure about your decision to refer to characters with the actors' names. It's clever but what does it achieve? It distracted me a bit from your argument.** who has identified the virus. They and the audience remember how fast it killed the people in Africa. Motava enters the body and multiplies so rapidly it kills within 24 hours. A movie released to the public is not the same like a book. **Seems too obvious to be worth stating.** A book can go on and on about one subject, **You are too conversational here for a formal essay.** but a movie has time limits and needs to have the attention of the audience long enough so that they do not walk out. The information presented in the movie was neither insufficient nor bring. **This must be some typo or distraction—doesn't make sense.** Since the beginning, it is imperative that *Outbreak* explains everything in the 128 minutes allotted.

The events in the book are more influenced by nature instead of man made like in the movie. The events that surround the Ebola Zaire strain in *The Hot Zone* are and remain mysterious. Ebola started as if, "it seemed to emerge out of the stillness of an implacable force brooding on an inscrutable intention" (p. 100). **Nice passage, good integration of this quotation.** Nature has a way of balancing itself. If Nature has to get humans, the "dominant species" to reduce its numbers she will do it. It makes sense the Ebola encounters humans with almost no signs. It is designed that way. By the time one person dies, it is already too late. The origin is also unknown. No film can capture that kind of an event. **How do you know this? Just** *because this film didn't accomplish it doesn't necessarily mean another film couldn't.* Outbreak had to infect one little town and get a vaccine to save dying people and add a tacked on military secret, which was an obstacle to get to the conclusion. That is the ideal situation for the American citizens to be saved and the people in Africa to die and suffer. *I'm lost. Help!* It would have been more realistic to let everyone infected die in the town, but then again René Russo had to be saved by her movie husband Dustin Hoffman.

The book itself had very little to do with the movie. *The Hot Zone* recounts the events between 1967 to 1993. The novel starts with the first known Ebola infected man and also tells about viruses, discusses Nature, and tells the events of African and American outbreaks. It would be literally impossible to put on the screen what is written in the novel. It is an informative piece of work that makes you paranoid after you have read what it can do. *Unclear. What is this "it" is referring to?* There is no rising action or climax. The conclusion is left for the reader to decide. *Could you try and be more specific here?* Outbreak had some real strong points but failed as a hard-core science fiction film. Watching Morgan Freeman selling out to the white man and the military meant that the movie only had a military message to offer with a nice coat of Motava to cover it up. It only foreshadowed what would happen if such a catastrophe were to happen.

Books are to be read, not to be made into multimillion-budgeted movies. Things *"Things" is such a catch-all, mean-nothing word. Can you find a better one?* are cut out to make a film convenient for the audience. What gets lost is the overall story, and flow. Books can take up as much space as they want, elaborate where necessary and give a sense of closure. Movies can only last so long and within that time they have to entertain, inform, and make a good lasting impression. It seems at first unfair because of the restrictions but, no one is really begging for a book to be made into a movie. *This is going to be a terrific essay, Arturo. I can feel how passionate you are about both the book and film. What you need to work on most is making your generalizations about how poorly the film conveyed the book's big ideas more concrete. Repeating that the film is weak isn't enough. Show how the book does it better.*

by Arturo Sernas

When "Awk" Isn't Enough

Most of us were taught to write—if we were taught to write at all—using a very different model than the one I am describing. Teachers assigned papers. We filled the required number of pages as best we could, and turned in the essay the following morning. The essay came back bleeding red ink and sprinkled with the standard teacher comments: "Unclear," "Repetitive," "Where is your topic sentence?" "Too much plot description." Our incompetence validated by the terse, negative, and unhelpful criticism, most of us decided that we agreed with the august teacher. We couldn't write. Her red pen proved it.

While a critical approach to teaching writing is meant to encourage good writing, it can sometimes discourage students forever. This is especially true for middle school students. Forgetting to include encouragement in our responses can also turn what should be an intellectually stimulating activity into a hateful task. This does not mean kids should be praised for turning in drivel or that the teacher should refrain from circling errors for fear of hurting students' feelings. Nothing is more damaging to an emerging writer than a vague "Well done!" on a paper that is full of spelling mistakes or punctuation errors. It's also dishonest. I want students to know that I believe with all my heart that with a bit more work they can be good writers, so I try to cast my criticism kindly:

- "I love your first sentence, Jorge. Continue with the metaphor. I want to know more about how you see this."
- "Please reread this essay for mechanical errors, Nathan. You don't want me to put a grade on the paper as is."
- "Anna, what do you think about including another quotation here? If you can't find one that works, how about another example? The point you are making is still a bit fuzzy."
- "I love this point, Rasheed, but it seems to me that it belongs at the beginning not the end of your paper. Try moving it and see if that works for you."
- "Help! This sentence makes no sense at all to me, Anna, as you have written here."

In *Everyone Can Write*, Peter Elbow explains how students benefit when they feel that writing is a transaction between human beings rather than an exercise in right or wrong.

> I try to make my comments on students' writing sound like they come from a human reader rather than from an impersonal machine or a magisterial, all-knowing God source. Thus:
>
> - Instead of saying "The organization is unclear here," I like to say "I got confused by your organization here."
> - Instead of "unconvincing," "I'm unconvinced."
> - Instead of "Diction," "Too slangy for me in this context."
> - Instead of "Awk," "I stumbled here" (2000, 359)

In his memoir on the craft, *On Writing*, Stephen King offers quirky but wise advice to young writers. One line of King's that I have taken up as my own when responding to student writing is "Adverbs are not your friends." If your students' papers resemble my students' papers, they are full of "reallys," "verys" and other excuses for weak verbs. King writes,

> Adverbs, like the passive voice, seem to have been created with the timid writer in mind. With the passive voice, the writer usually expresses fear of not being taken seriously; it is the voice of little boys wearing shoe polish mustaches and little girls clumping around in Mommy's high heels. With adverbs, the writer usually tells us he or she is afraid he/she isn't expressing himself/herself clearly, that he or she is not getting the point or picture across. (2000, 124)

The statement, "Adverbs are not your friends," helps me say to students that what they have written isn't incorrect but rather imprecise. Good writers know to search for that active verb that will make readers sit up and take notice.

Like King, the inimitable E. B. White also admonishes writers to avoid the use of qualifiers. "*Rather, very, little, pretty*—these are the leeches that infest the pond of prose, sucking the blood of words" (Strunk and White 2000, 73). White enjoins us to write with nouns

is more likely to focus too soon on technique. A student, moreover, may write off the comments of a teacher by saying to himself, "Adults just can't understand," or "English teachers are nit-pickers anyway," but when his fellow human beings misread him, he has to accommodate the feedback. By habitually responding and coaching, students get insights about their own writing. They become much more involved both in writing and in reading what others have written. (1968, 195)

I love the way Moffett assumes that students don't consider their English teachers "human beings." He's probably right. It reminds me of when my son was in middle school and I was beside myself over his spelling. He knew the difference between *there* and *their* and about *i* before *e* except after *c* but could never be bothered to employ what he knew in his writing. Though my face grew red from shouting, James would shrug and say, "Relax." Nothing makes an obsessive mother turn more red in the face than being told by a twelve-year-old to "relax." It wasn't until he got involved in online chat rooms—the ones where the middle school–age participants pretend to be college students—that he suddenly began putting what he knew in theory into practice. A girl, probably herself not more than twelve, told him that she didn't believe he was a freshman at UCLA. "Why you can't even spell!" Almost overnight, James started applying what he knew about correctness to his writing. He saw that proper spelling wasn't just something his ancient teachers expected but rather something the world expected. If he hoped to be taken seriously, he needed to get it right.

Students offer one another a wholly different response than their teacher offers, and young writers need both. Another way to model students' peer responses is to ask for a volunteer to share a work in progress in front of the class and, with clarifying questions, help refine the problems student readers encounter in the draft. Because student listeners have a difficult time taking in a whole essay read aloud, I ask the writer to stop after each paragraph. I begin by asking the writer what feedback he or she is looking for. In this way the conversation is

GRAMMAR CRIME HOT SHEET

1. **Failure to underline book titles**

   Titles that should be underlined or italicized (if you have a computer that will italicize) include: books, book-length poems, plays, magazines, pamphlets, published speeches, long musical works, movies, television programs, works of visual art (titles of paintings, statues, etc.), ships, and foreign phrases.

   Titles that should be in quotation marks are: short stories, songs, short poems, articles in magazines, essays, episodes of a television program, and chapter titles in a book.

   Correct examples: book: *The Giver*; short story: "Little Red Riding Hood"; short poem: "Ozymandias"; long poem: *The Song of Roland*; movie: *Men in Black*

2. **Speeding through contractions**

   Never, never, never write: *should of, could of, would of.*

   The correct way: *should have, could have, would have*

   The correct contraction: *should've, could've, would've*

   Correct example: The boy should've been nicer to his sister.

   By the way, try to avoid using contractions in formal writing, please!

3. **Illicit use of the word *like***

   Avoid the use of the word *like* at all costs when you are using it to cite examples.

   Replace like with *such as, for example, for instance.*

4. **Use of forbidden, boring, informal words**

   From now on, these words are forbidden in formal writing in this classroom: *a lot, all right, stuff, well, gonna, wanna, kinda*

   (of course, the last three words can be used in their correct format: *going to, want to, kind of*).

5. **Incorrect spelling**

   These words are commonly misspelled at this school: *beginning, choose, chose, loose, lose,* and *separate.*

6. **Improper matching of *they* to *their*, and *he/she* to *his/her***

   If the beginning of the sentence says: The mother wanted to make the boy happy, then the rest should say: so she gave her favorite old toy to him.

   Make sure the descriptive words *their, his, her* refer to the correct subject.

   If the subject is a single thing (such as a thing, a person, etc.), then don't use *their.*

7. **Illegal use of *because* and *until***

   If you want to use *because* and *until*, then use the complete form of the word.

   Never use *cause* or *til.* (Note: Sometimes you will see *till* used in poems and advertisements.)

   The correct contractions for these words are *'cause* and *'til.* Avoid using contractions in formal writing.

8. **Mixing up *this, that,* and *who***

   Never say: There was this boy and this tree . . . Correct example: There was a boy and a tree . . .

   Only use *this* when the thing is right there in front of you.

   Never say: The story is about a young boy that loves a tree.

   Use *who* when referring to people. The boy is a person, so the sentence should read: The story is about a young boy who loves a tree.

   Use *that* for objects and things, not people.

   (continued)

9. **Illegal use of *it's* and *its***
   Correct examples: It's the right thing to do. (contraction for "it is")
   The building cast its shadow. (The shadow belongs to the building, so its is a possessive, and doesn't use an apostrophe! Most other possessives use an apostrophe: John's book, Joe's shoe.)

10. **Illegal use of *your* and *you're***
    Everyone spells these alike because they sound alike. BEWARE!!!!
    Correct examples: You're almost ready to try it alone. (contraction for "you are")
    Here is your paper. (*your* is a possessive, the paper belongs to you)

11. **Illegal use of *their* and *there* and *they're***
    Three more words that everyone spells the same because they sound the same. Correct examples:
    There is another door over there. (shows location or existence)
    Their ice cream cones are melting all over their shoes. (possessive)
    They're not really ready to go yet. (contraction for "they are")
    Set an alarm in your brain that goes off every time you are about to use one of these words, and make sure to stop and check that you are using the correct form before you go on.

12. **Illegal use of *s*/illegal use of the apostrophe**
    An *s* is put at the end of a word for two reasons: to make it plural or to show possession.
    Correct examples: Plurals: books, students; Possession: the book's pages, the student's desk.
    When you add an *s* to make something plural, *do not use* an apostrophe. (Note: the only exception is shown in Grammar Crime No. 9 above.)

13. **Illegal use of *to*, *too*, and *two***
    Use *too* when you are exaggerating. Example: It was too much!
    Too can also mean *also*. Example: I want to go too!
    Two means the numeral 2.
    Correct example: I want to go too so I can buy two pieces of candy.

14. **Improper matching of verbs**
    If the subject of the sentence is singular, use a singular verb.
    Examples: It walks, rides, was, is, says, tries, decides, spoke, can, will, does.
    If the subject of the sentence is plural, then use a verb that goes with the plural. Example: They walk, ride, were, are, say, try, decide, spoke, can, will, do

15. **Using double negatives**
    In other languages, such as Spanish, the more negatives you have in a sentence, the more negative the statement. But in English, you can have only one negative per sentence, so make sure you don't put more than one of these words in the same sentence:
    Negatives: *not, don't, can't, won't, shouldn't, couldn't, wouldn't, didn't, no, neither, nothing*
    Here is an example of too many negatives from a student paper: Having no trees aren't nothing. (There are three negatives in that above sentence!)

16. **Mixing up *will* and *can*, *would* and *could***
    If you are writing in the present tense, use verbs such as *are*, *is*, or *does*. Then when you want to use the future tense, use *will* or *can*.
    If you are writing in the past tense, use verbs such as *were*, *was*, or *did*. Then when you want to use the future tense, use *would* or *could*.

© 2002 by Carol Jago from *Cohesive Writing*. Portsmouth, NH: Heinemann.

FIGURE 5–3 *Grammatical crime hot sheet*

Peer Response Sheet
Book and Film Comparison Draft

Your name: _____

Writer's name: _____

Today's date: _____

1. Does the essay's title entice you to read on? **Yes/ No** If no, please suggest a better one.

_____

2. Underline what you believe to be the writer's thesis statement. Are the book title, author's name, and movie title all mentioned in the first paragraph? **Yes/No**

3. List here the writer's main points of comparison and contrast:

_____

_____

_____

4. Did the writer develop his/her analysis of these points sufficiently? Explain.

_____

5. Check transitions between paragraphs. Are they effective or could they be improved? Make suggestions.

_____

6. What do you think are the two best things about this essay? Be very specific (not "I liked it a lot").

_____

7. Staple this paper to your partner's draft and offer the writer further assistance.

© 2002 by Carol Jago from *Cohesive Writing*. Portsmouth, NH: Heinemann.

FIGURE 5–4 *Peer response sheet*

immediately focused on the issues the writer cares most about. Then I might say:

- "Aileen just said that she thinks her opening paragraph is boring. Let's take a look at the lengths of her sentences in that paragraph. Are they all short or all long? How could she alter this?"
- "Jorge, you say that Aileen's last sentence is clumsy and hard to understand. Where exactly in the sentence did you stumble? Can you think of a simpler or more straightforward way to phrase it without changing her meaning?"
- "Aileen thinks her word choice is too babyish. Can anyone think of another verb she could use instead of 'get'? Where else could her diction be made more precise?"
- "What does Aileen do really well here?" (I am always careful to end the session with positive strokes for the writer.)

This group session helps students turn their vague responses into useful technical advice for the writer. Once they see that they won't be pilloried for their mistakes, students are often keen to have their drafts scrutinized by the whole class.

Inevitably there are times when my tidy five-day plan falls apart. Surprise pep assemblies, student body election meetings, counseling appointments, and various other interruptions seem to conspire against coherent classroom instruction. Once when my Day Four plan for peer revision was blown apart by a student performance of *Grease!* I came up with the following take-home form (Figure 5–5).

I have also used the following letter (Figure 5–6) to encourage feedback from home. Many of my students speak languages other than English at home and may have no one at home who can read their paper. Students have solved this problem by translating and paraphrasing their writing for a parent or by seeking help from brothers or sisters who speak English. As the letter makes clear, the purpose of having writers share their work in this manner is not to obtain editing assistance but for response to content. Parents of teenagers are often delighted to be included in their children's schoolwork.

Writers Need Readers

Tonight's homework assignment is to have your draft read by three caring readers. You may solicit readers from among family or friends (no pets!). If no one is at home, you may read your draft to someone over the phone or email it to a willing correspondent. Whenever possible, have your readers sign here:

I certify that I have read the attached essay and talked with the writer about how it could be improved.

Reader 1: _____

Reader 2: _____

Reader 3: _____

© 2002 by Carol Jago from *Cohesive Writing*. Portsmouth, NH: Heinemann.

FIGURE 5–5 *Writers need readers*

Authentic Revision

Peer response exercises also open the door to lessons on revision techniques that benefit the whole class. After we worked with Aileen's draft, I asked everyone to draw pencil lines between each of their sentences, checking to see if a lack of sentence variety might also be contributing to their draft's monotonous tone. Partners then took time to work on combining short, choppy sentences into longer, complex ones and to break up any paragraphs full of complex prose with a pithy short sentence.

Another aspect of student drafts to focus on is the opening sentence. We have begun a class collection of the "all-time worsts":

"Different experiences in a person's life are what shape who they are."

"It is hard to pinpoint human nature."

"All good novels always have an underlying message."

Santa Monica High School
601 Pico Boulevard #102
Pacific Palisades, CA 90272

October 8, 2001

Dear Friend of the Writer,

I invite you to take a look at this draft and talk with the writer about what you see and hear. This is not a finished copy but a working version of the essay. To make it better, the writer needs feedback from readers.

In an open letter to parents, the National Council of Teachers of English states:

> Be as helpful as you can when your children write. Talk through their ideas with them; help them discover what they want to say. When they ask for help with spelling, punctuation, and usage, supply that help. Your most effective role is not as a critic but as a helper. Rejoice in effort, delight in ideas, and resist the temptation to be critical.

Please sign here that you have shared your thoughts about this paper with your child or friend:

_____

Signature

_____

Date

Thank you for taking the time to do this. I know it makes a difference.

Sincerely,

Carol Jago

Carol Jago

FIGURE 5–6 *Letters home*

"Throughout life, we all come across obstacles in which we have to make very critical decisions."

"Every book is made up of words."

Every one of these sentences was written by a student. We talk about how such sentences can be a means of getting one's fingers moving on the keyboard but how in revision they need to be eliminated or replaced. It seems to me that what students are often stretching for with such pompous opening statements is a way to lend significance to the essay that follows. I assure them that vague generalizations about life and literature will sooner put their readers to sleep than prepare them for insightful analysis. Pointing this out to young writers usually weans them of this bad habit right away. Keeping a running list of "Pompous Opening Sentences" posted can also help students remember to avoid such terrible writing.

Novice writers also tend to fill and end their sentences with limp prepositional phrases. Some of this is the novice writer's natural tendency to qualify and requalify everything rather than make confident statements. I tell students that if a sentence had a dollar value, its first few words would be worth a buck, the middle about twenty-five cents, and the end a whopping ten dollars. When writers end a sentence with prepositional phrases, they don't take advantage of the punch a well-constructed sentence can deliver and their sentense loses currency. Instead of writing "The reader gets a very strong image that they will remain together for the rest of the chapter," a better rendering of this thought might be, "Throughout the chapter, we have a sense that the characters will stay together." I ask students to find a sentence in their draft that ends in a prepositional phrase and identify the sentence's most powerful word. We then try to revise it for impact.

Clearly Day Four can be extended to several days of work. You need to judge the extent to which any particular group of students has the patience for additional revision. Once I feel students have had enough, we move on. We can deal with other revision techniques in their next essay.

Self-Assessment

Along with collecting papers on Day Five, I use this class period to have students decide for themselves how well they feel they have met the challenges of this particular writing task. I ask them to write for ten minutes and tell me this essay's story. Where did the thesis idea originate? What do they like best about the paper? What obstacles barred their way? How well does the final product meet their expectations? Are there any mitigating factors that influenced their work for better or for worse? What do they plan to do next time? This metacognitive moment gives me an insight into students' development as writers.

Another way to help students think about the changes they have made from draft to final copy is to have them fill out a form like the one in Figure 5–7.

All this attention to revision and process results in papers like Emilie's (see below). While not perfect, her essay is a fine example of outstanding cohesive writing. I spend very little time with students' final papers, simply stapling a copy of the rubric to the back and highlighting appropriate phrases within the scoring guide. Emilie's rubric was marked as follows:

Santa Monica High School English Department
Analytical Essay Scoring Guide, Grades 9–12

6: A **6** paper presents an *insightful analysis* of the text, elaborating with *well-chosen examples* and *persuasive reasoning*. It has *mature development and style*. The 6 paper shows that its writer can use a variety of *sophisticated sentences* effectively, observe the conventions of written English, and *choose words aptly*.

Using our department's scoring guide in this fashion is a shortcut. I would prefer to write a more detailed and personal response to Emilie congratulating her on her hard work and pointing out exactly where her prose soared. Unfortunately, with the number of students I teach, this is simply not possible. I need to find a balance between sacrificing my own life—including my reading life—to student papers and offering

Evaluating Your Revision

Reread your draft and your revision. Then answer the following questions:

1. What changes did you make from draft to revision?

_____

_____

_____

2. How did these changes improve your essay?

_____

_____

_____

3. What do you like best about your revised work?

_____

_____

_____

4. What would you continue to work on if you had more time?

_____

_____

_____

5. What else do you want me to know before reading your paper?

_____

_____

_____

FIGURE 5–7 *Evaluating your revision*

students the critical assistance they need. Often I am able to find the time to write detailed commentaries on final copies; I just don't beat myself up when it is not possible. Too many good teachers have left the profession over the paper load. Given the imperfect world we live in, I believe it is more valuable if I focus my critical eye on students' drafts than on their final products.

Final Copy
Point Method
Simple Minds

In Jerzy Kozinski's *Being There*, the main character Chance cannot understand what is outside his home and his garden. He is disconnected from the normal human thought process and is therefore often confused by emotions and social structure. In the movie *Forest Gump*, a similar character is portrayed by Forest, who, unlike Chance, does understand emotions and relationships on a basic level, but doesn't always see the complete truth because of his idealistic thinking. They are like children because they are both naïve and unaware of many conventions of society.

Because Forest's mental disability is apparent to everybody but Chance's goes unnoticed, society gives them completely different status. Forest is viewed as a retard and is constantly taken for less than what he is. Kids throw rocks at him and he has a hard time getting into normal school. Whenever his is talented at something like running or he makes the college football team, it is only talked about as a freak—like he is so stupid he can't do anything but run. Chance, on the other hand, is given everything. He is immediately accepted into the highest society by the Rand couple and every little thing he says is taken as a metaphor for life. While being interviewed on a news talk show, the host recaps his interpretation of the conversation: "It is your view, then that the slowing of the economy . . . is just another phase, another season, so to speak, in the growth of a garden" (67). The host thinks that Chance is speaking about the economy by comparing it to a garden, when Chance is talking about the garden not as a metaphor for the economy, but because that's the only part of the question he understands and so he went on about the growth in an actual garden.

Both Chance and Forest's lives greatly affect society, but Forest is actively trying to accomplish something whereas Chance just lets life happen and luckily he is often in the right place at the right time. Forest's main goal in life is to be extremely dedicated to his friends. Forest wins the Congressional Medal of Honor and meets the President for saving his troop in Vietnam. He then starts Bubba-Gump Shrimp company all by himself because of his promise to his friend Bubba. Both of these things took independence and dedication. Chance doesn't do anything from his own initiative. He was never even curious enough to try and find out what was beyond his garden and room. When he isn't allowed to live in his house anymore, he just takes a walk and happens to fall into the hands of the right people, who introduce him to the President. He answers everyone's questions with complete ignorance, and they interpret his statements to mean what they want.

Chance and Forest see life completely differently—Forest sees good versus evil and tries to be an ethical person, while Chance just sees actions without any thought as to whether they are good or bad. When Forest goes to a nightclub to see Jenny sing a man grabs her foot. Jenny likes it because it means she has fans and is wanted, but Forest thinks he is trying to hurt her, so he carries her off the stage in an attempt to rescue her. Even though his effort was misconstrued, his purpose was good. Also, in general Forest's narrative voice expresses excitement and happiness or sorrow, but Chance is never affected emotionally by anything that happens. He isn't happy about what political power he has, and he is not excited by women nor disturbed by gay men. He is mostly confused by all of these emotions. He watches TV to see what the correct actions are in specific situations, but he doesn't understand the feeling behind the actions.

Forest tries extremely hard to do the right thing in life and gets emotionally involved in life. Chance just floats through life without a purpose and goes along with whatever people suggest. Forest is isolated from society on the outside because they won't accept him because of his disability, and Chance is isolated from society on the inside because he doesn't understand human emotions. They both have relatively simple minds, but Forest applies himself and makes the best of his situation. Chance just exists and society makes everything up themselves. Two men with disabilities make more positive changes in the nation than most of the population, which shows how much one life can do.

by Emilie Phelps

It is important that students reflect on each essay as they hand it in, as well as on their writing over a period of time. In my experience this is the most powerful reason for students to keep portfolios. Throughout the course of the year I ask students to keep track of what they file in their portfolios (see Figure 5–8). I also have students keep track of the books they read over the course of the year. The running log (see Figure 5–9) seems to help them feel a sense of accomplishment regarding their class work and provides documentary evidence of their reading lives. In January students read through their portfolios—including selected work from previous years—and complete a portfolio self-assessment (see Figure 5–10).

In a variation of the culminating self-assessment assignment in June I ask students to look through their portfolios and choose an essay that clearly needs revision. I tell students that they are not going to have to revise the paper but instead write a letter to me explaining what they would do if they were to rewrite.

Dear Mrs. Jago,

I've learned some important things since I wrote my very first essay of the year, "A Fatherly Figure." One mistake I made in this essay was to make my opening line self-important. I now know it is better to have no opening and no closing line rather than a pompous one.

I was also surprised at how unclear a lot of my analysis of the quotes could be. For instance, in the first paragraph, after the words "wreak harm on him," I could not see how my explanation in any way related to the thesis. It leads the reader to a dead end that leaves them confused.

My paragraphs are really long and make my head spin. They're too messy. There is a sort of choppiness to the writing instead of a continual flow leading up to a point. For a long while I explain things without telling what point has been made, which

Portfolio Checklist

Type of writing	Title of paper	Paper's strengths	Paper's weaknesses

© 2002 by Carol Jago from *Cohesive Writing*. Portsmouth, NH: Heinemann.

FIGURE 5–8 *Portfolio checklist*

Reading Log		
Title	Author	Date completed

FIGURE 5–9   *Reading log*

Portfolio Self-Assessment
January, _____

Instructions: Put all of your work in chronological order. Read through the pieces in your portfolio. Review the comments I have made on each one. Please respond thoughtfully to each of these questions.

1. Based upon my comments and those of your peers, what are the strengths in your writing? What do **you** perceive as your strengths in writing?

2. Based upon my comments and those of your peers, what are the weaknesses in your writing? What do **you** perceive as your weaknesses in writing?

3. What continues to be your greatest challenge as a writer? Cite a specific example here.

4. What growth do you see in yourself as a writer since September? Do you see growth as a reader as well? Explain.

5. What goals do you plan to set for yourself as a writer for second semester? Please be more specific and more thoughtful than "Improve my spelling."

6. Select the one essay that you consider to be the best example of your writing. What made this essay successful? What are you proud of having accomplished here? Title of essay:_____

Please staple the essay to your responses.

© 2002 by Carol Jago from *Cohesive Writing*. Portsmouth, NH: Heinemann.

FIGURE 5–10 *Portfolio self-assessment*

leaves the reader handing and lost. I also learned to try not to use contractions too much, especially when I need to make an impact.

Sincerely,
Rachel Greenberg

Dear Mrs. Jago,

I picked my last essay because I spent the least time on it, but it still turned out all right. I think I was able to get my points across but unfortunately a lot of the style was lost. My frequent grammatical errors also took away from the flow of the essay. In your comments you pointed out that it would be more powerful if it were more concise. I definitely would like to be able to write exactly what I want the first time, but it usually takes me a few sentences to get down what I had in mind. This again probably could be solved with better revising, or in this case any revising. My title sucks and my opening paragraph is weak but the content is there. It's just ugly.

Michael Egziabher

Dear Mrs. Jago,

As I reflect on my process piece on *The Bell Jar,* I can see many changes and improvements I would make. The quality of the essay both shows in the grade, and in the content. The content of my essay reflects a certain lack of focus I had during the writing of the essay. Before I actually began writing, I spent a lot of time drawing my thoughts together to devise an insightful thesis. The book really drew me in and inspired more thinking in me, yet this didn't extend to my essay writing. While the ideas were thriving inside my mind, I found it difficulty to make the transfer from thought to words. This sense of frustration and uncertainty came out in my writing. The ideas I explored in the analysis were strong, but came out unclear and awkward. The connection between my analysis and thesis was ownften not concrete or clear. My ideas did not flow as freely as they did in my mind. I think this mental block was prominent in many of my earlier essays. I think that I have improved over the year in being able to focus and organize my thoughts on paper. If I were to rewrite it, I think just the fact that I have grown as a writer would bring improvements. I now understand my lack of focus during the process of writing the essay. I believe that in understanding those faults, I am able to focus more on improvement.

Sincerely,
Aimee Oyenoki

How students develop as writers to a great extent depends on my ability to stimulate reflection on their own writing. To my mind Rachel's, Michael's, and Aimee's responses indicate that they have a clear idea about what cohesive writing should look like. Of course it is important to point out where students have gone wrong and how they might do better, but teachers shouldn't forget the power they wield with their red pens. Writing mentors can use this power to prove that they know more than students about spelling and punctuation, or they can use it to guide. With apologies to William Carlos Williams,

> so much depends
> upon
>
> a red exclamation
> point
>
> telling you
> Yes!
>
> this is good
> writing.

SIX

Ω

Cohesive Writing Matters

Teaching students to write cohesively requires a cohesive instructional plan. The preceding chapters outline a method that I have found successful for helping students produce coherent essays. Some readers may feel that my way of working with students is too directive, preferring the discovery approach to good writing. While I recognize the importance of helping students find their voices as writers, my experience with teenagers, particularly with unskilled writers, has been that their voices emerge more readily once certain basics have been mastered. Rather than chafing at my directions, many students seem to be relieved. As André said to me in Chapter 2, "Why did nobody ever tell me this before? My last year's teacher just kept putting us in groups and telling us to help each other. We're kids. How're we supposed to know what to do? Teachers should teach."

One of the things a good teacher teaches students is how to work within a group, but that doesn't mean abrogating our responsibility to instruct. As Lisa Delpit explains in *Other People's Children,*

Although the problem is not necessarily inherent in the method, in some instances adherents of process approaches to writing create situations in which students ultimately find themselves held accountable for knowing a set of rules about which no one has ever directly informed them. Teachers do students no service to suggest, even implicitly, that "product" is not important. In this country students will be judged on their product regardless of the process they

117

utilized to achieve it. And that product, based as it is on the specific codes of a particular culture, is more readily produced when the directives of how to produce it are made explicit.

If such explicitness is not provided to students, what it feels like to people who are old enough to judge is that there are secrets being kept, that time is being wasted, that the teacher is abdicating his or her duty to teach. (1995, 31)

I agree. For some students, an English teacher is their only source for information about how to write cohesively. Writing instructors must do more than facilitate. They must teach. To determine what is most important to teach, I return to my core beliefs:

1. In order to learn to write, one must write.
2. Authentic tasks and topics generate the most cohesive student writing.
3. Students need both supportive and critical feedback.
4. There is no cohesive writing without revision.

If I want my students to write extensively, I am going to have to assign a series of papers. While inviting students to write as the spirit moves them may work in a creative writing class, typical ninth-grade students are more like Bartelby. When asked to write, they cheerfully reply: "I should prefer not to."

If I want to generate cohesive writing from students, I need to work hard to create authentic and cohesive prompts that pique their interest and offer them space to explore within manageable boundaries. Giving students a total choice of topics has never worked for me. At the same time, straightjacket prompts with little room for individual expression are also deadly. Finding a balance between too much and too little freedom in writing assignments is something I struggle with daily and expect to continue to do so. Often it is a student who discovers something that is not quite right in one of my prompts. I welcome such feedback and am quick to bring the class's attention to what must have been giving many of them trouble. It shocks students that I should do this, but I remind them that I really am on their side.

If I want students to write cohesively, they are going to need both supportive and critical feedback. I expect that students will make mistakes and that they will need my help. This is my job. While encouraging students to write expressively and to begin establishing their own voices, I am also forthright about where their voices falter as a result of incoherence or inaccuracy. With Lisa Delpit I believe that "pretending that gatekeeping points don't exist is to ensure that many students will not pass through them" (39). I mark errors in red and tell students when a paper needs to be completely redone. Shabby work is unacceptable. At the same time, I try to phrase my criticism in terms that suggest it is the work, not the child, who is flawed.

Students will never write cohesively until they accept that revision is a natural part of writing. To teach them this, I must structure writing lessons that hold students accountable for the generation of a draft, extensive revision and editing, and a final polished copy. Though it might make you crazy to hear this, I always allow students to rewrite their final papers. To my mind this is a genuinely teachable moment. Any student so dissatisfied with a grade that he or she will find the time to step back and revise an essay while the class moves on to the next assignment deserves the chance to do so. Yes, it is a bookkeeping nightmare for the teacher, but for some students this final revision is a moment of significant growth.

Cohesive writing matters. I want my students to produce prose that is "harmoniously accordant," that hangs together, and that communicates their ideas coherently. Without this skill, they will be forever relegated to secondary status as students. With it, the world is their oyster.

Bibliography

ATWAN, ROBERT. 1995. *The Best American Essays*. New York: Houghton Mifflin.

BLAIR, HUGH. 1965. *Lectures on Rhetoric and Belles Lettres* (Edinburgh, 1783), in the facsimile edited by Harold F. Harding. Carbondale, IL: Southern Illinois Unversity Press.

COLORADO UNCENSORED CONFERENCE. 2001. *www.coloradouncensored.org*.

COTICH, CRAIG, AND JOAN COTICH. 2001. "Be Careful What You Ask For." *California English* 6(5): 9–11.

DELPIT, LISA. 1995. *Other People's Children*. New York: The New Press.

ELBOW, PETER. 2000. *Everyone Can Write*. New York: Oxford University Press.

EPSTEIN, JOSEPH. 1997. *The Norton Book of Personal Essays*. New York: W.W. Norton.

GARDNER, JOHN. 1991. *The Art of Fiction: Notes on Craft for Young Writers*. New York: Vintage Books.

HOAGLAND, EDWARD, ed. 1999. *The Best Essays 1999*. New York: Houghton Mifflin.

HOFF, DAVID J. 2001. "Well-Crafted Assignments Key to Good Writing, Researchers Find." *Education Week*, 11 July, 5.

KING, STEPHEN. 2000. *On Writing: A Memoir of the Craft*. New York: Scribner.

LAMOTT, ANNE. 1994. *Bird by Bird: Some Instructions on Writing and Life*. New York: Pantheon Books.

LeCren, Carole. 1998. "Grammar Crimes? Do the Time!" *California English* 39(3): 22–23.

Moffett, James. 1968. *Teaching the Universe of Discourse*. Boston: Houghton Mifflin Company.

Payne, Michele. 2000. *Bodily Discourse: When Students Write About Abuse and Eating Disorders*. Portsmouth, NH: Boynton/Cook.

Rosenblatt, Roger. 1994. *The Man in the Water*. New York: Random House.

Stafford, William. 1978. *Writing the Australian Crawl*. Ann Arbor, MI: University of Michigan Press.

Strunk Jr., William, and E. B. White. 2000. *The Elements of Style*. New York: Allyn & Bacon.

U.S. Department of Education. Office of Educational Research and Improvement, National Center for Education Statistics. 1999. *The NAEP Writing Report Card for the Nation and the States*, NCES 199–462, by E. A. Greenwald, H. R. Persky, J. R. Campbell, and J. Mazzeo. Washington, DC.

Wisconsin's Model Academic Standards for English Language Arts. 1998. Madison, WI: Wisconsin Department of Public Instruction.

Wolff, Tobias. 1994. *In Pharoah's Army, Memoirs of the Lost War*. New York: Vintage Books.

Woodward, Katherine. 1999. *Alignment of National and State Standards, A Report by the GED Testing Service*. Washington, DC: American Council on Education.

About the Author

Carol Jago teaches English at Santa Monica High School in Santa Monica, California, and directs the California Reading and Literature Project at UCLA. She also edits the California Association of Teachers of English quarterly journal, *California English*. Carol has written a weekly education column for the *Los Angeles Times*, and her essays have appeared in *English Journal*, *Language Arts*, *NEA Today*, *The Christian Science Monitor*, as well as in other newspapers across the nation. She is the author of *Nikki Giovanni in the Classroom*, *Alice Walker in the Classroom*, *Sandra Cisneros in the Classroom* (NCTE), *With Rigor for All: Teaching the Classics to Contemporary Students*, and *Beyond Standards: Excellence in the High School English Classroom*.

Ω

Index

abuse, student writing about, 48–49
academic achievement, 5
active verbs, 96
adverbs, 96
Aldrich, Marcia, 25
Alignment of National and State Standards (Woodward), 1
"all-time worsts," 104, 106
American plain style, 97
analytic writing
    instruction in, 67
    six-point rubrics, 68
Analyzing a Published Essay (form), 26
arguments, refutation of, 36
Art of Fiction, The: Notes on Craft for Young Writers (Gardner), 52
art prints, writing dialogue from, 52
assessment
    grading, 61–67
    holistic, 66, 67
    multiple traits scoring, 66–67
    NAEP, 1, 2, 35–38
    of quickwrites, 86–87
    self-, 106–16
Atwan, Robert, 24
Atwood, Margaret, 12
"Aunt Jennifer's Tigers" (Rich), 12
Austen, Jane, 88
authentic prompts, 36–37, 118
authentic responses to literature, 81
authentic revision, 104–6
authors, using writing styles of, 80
autobiographical narratives. See also narrative writing
    California Standards Test Scoring Rubric, 62–66
    college essays, 53–59

Being There (Kozinski), 88, 109–11
Bell Jar, The (Plath), 14–15, 115
Best American Essays, The (Atwan, 1995), 24
Best Essays of 1999, The (Hoagland), 24
biographical narratives, 55
Bird by Bird: Some Instructions on Writing and Life (Lamott), 8
Bladerunner, 88
Blair, Hugh, 84
block method, 89–90
Bodily Discourse: When Students Write About Abuse and Eating Disorders (Payne), 49
Boyle, T. C., 72–73
Britton, James, 1
Bryon, Lord, 10–11

California High School Exit Exam
    four-point rubric, 62
    Response to Literary/Expository Text, 61
California Standards Test Scoring Rubric, 62–66
Cather, Willa, 20–21
characters
    imagining in different situations, 80
    writing about favorites, 80–81
    writing exercises, 51, 52
choice
    importance of, 25
    of writing topics, 30–31
cinema. See movies
class discussion, writing before, 30
clichés, 97
Clueless, 88
coaches, teachers as, 97
Cofer, Judith Ortiz, 25
cohesion, 7
cohesive writing. See also writing

authentic revision, 104–6
  criticism and, 119
  defined, 7
  encouraging, 95–97
  five-day writing plan, 87–94
  importance of, 117–18
  mechanical errors and, 97–98
  method, 7–21
  models of, 23–24
  obstacles to, 83
  peer response and, 98–99, 102–4
  revision and, 119
  self-assessment, 107–16
  student understanding of, 116
  thinking and, 83–85
  writing process and, 83–85
  writing volume and, 83–84, 85–87
College Board
  AP Language and AP Literature prompts, 20
  rubrics, 66
college essays, 53–59
  "best," 56
  biographical narratives, 55
  epiphanies, 56
  examples, 56–59
  highlighting personal qualities in, 54–55
  issues, 55–56
  length of, 54, 55
  samples, 56–59
  time line for, 54–55
comparison/contrast papers, 88–94
  organizing, 88–90
  teacher criticism of, 91–94
Cotich, Craig, 16
Cotich, Joan, 16
crayons, marking essays with, 30
creative fiction. *See* narrative writing
criticism
  of comparison/contrast papers, 91–94
  effectiveness of, 95, 119
  encouragement and, 95–97
  of narrative writing, 39
  student response to, 117
  time for, 107, 109
  value of, 119
culminating assignments, 80–81

Death of a Salesman (Miller), 79
definition essays, 15–16
Delpit, Lisa, 117–18, 119
dialogue writing exercise, 53
Dick, Philip K., 88
directions, in writing prompts, 18
Do Androids Dream of Electric Sheep? (Dick), 88
Doctorow, E. L., 8
drafting

freewriting *vs.*, 13
  as homework, 91
  in-class, 91
  moving from question papers to, 13–14
drafts
  as final products, 84
  sending via e-mail, 92
  writing conferences about, 33–34

editing. *See also* revision
  peer, 98–99, 102–4
editorials
  news stories *vs.*, 32
  selecting from newspapers, 31
Educational Testing Service, 15
Elbow, Peter, 1, 86, 96
Elements of Style (Strunk and White), 97
e-mail, for sending drafts, 92
Emma (Austen), 88
encouragement, 95–97
epiphanies, 56
Epstein, Joseph, 23, 27, 28
essays
  college, 53–59
  defined, 38
  definition, 15–16
  encouraging students to try, 38
  organic nature of, 30
  personal, 23
  persuasive, 30–38
  quality of, 35
  reading, 23
  thousand-word, 8–9
essays (professional)
  choice in reading, 25
  deconstructing, 27–28
  development in, 27
  finding thesis in, 25
  marking with crayons, 30
  as models, 23–25
  purpose of, 25, 27
  reading, 24–25
  small-group reading of, 25
  topics for, 27–28
Evaluating Your Revision (form), 108
events, ordering, 52–53
Everyone can Write (Elbow), 96
evidence, for thesis, 25, 30
expository writing, 31–32
  freewriting *vs.*, 13

feedback. *See also* criticism
  from parents, 103–4
fictional narratives. *See also* narrative writing
  California Standards Test Scoring Rubric, 62–66
fictional worlds, writing about, 80

films. *See* movies
"find-the-thesis" task, 25
five-day writing plan, 88–94
    Day One, 89–90
    Day Two, 89, 90–91
    Day Three, 89, 91
    Day Four, 89, 91, 103, 106
    Day Five, 89, 107
"Flowers for Algernon" (Keyes), 86
Forester, E. M., 31
Forest Gump, 88
forms
    Analyzing a Published Essay, 26
    Evaluating Your Revision, 108
    Portfolio Checklist, 112
    Portfolio Self-Assessment, 114
    Reading Log, 113
    Writers Need Readers, 104
four-point rubric, 63–66
freewriting
    drafting *vs.*, 13
    for overcoming inertia, 9
    question papers as, 13

Gardner, John, 52
GED Testing Service, 1
generalizations, 106
Gentile, Claudia, 15–16
Gettysburg Address (Lincoln), 84
Ginsberg, Allen, 87
Gotswami, Dixie, 1
grading. *See also* assessment; self-assessment
    multiple traits scoring, 66–67
    rubrics, 61–66
Graham, Carol Shaw, 61–62
grammar
    guidelines, 98, 100–101
    mechanical errors, 5–6, 97–98
Grammar Crime Hot Sheet, 98, 100–101
Graves, Donald, 1
Gray, James, 1
Great Gatsby, The (Fitzgerald), 78

"Hair" (Aldrich), 25
high-stakes writing assignments, 88
Hoagland, Edward, 24
Hodgman, Ann, 25
holistic assessment, 66, 67
homework
    drafts as, 91
    writing-to-learn papers about, 87
Hot Zone, The (Preston), 88, 92–94
"Howl" (Ginsberg), 87
"How to Get Out of a Locked Trunk" (Weiss), 24
Hunger of Memory (Rodriquez), 67, 69–72

"If the River Was Whiskey" (Boyle), 72–73
in-class writing assignments, 85–86, 91
indefinite pronouns, 97
inertia exercises, 9
informational writing, 31–32
    persuasive writing *vs.*, 32
In Pharoah's Army, Memoirs of the Lost War (Wolff), 61
Iowa, University of, Writer's Workshop, 85
irony, 36

Jago, Carol, 28–30
James, Patrick, 56
Joy Luck Club, The (Tan), 13–14
Julius Caesar (Shakespeare), 86

Keyes, Daniel, 86
King, Stephen, 96
Kingston, Maxine Hong, 74, 75–77
Kozinski, Jerzy, 88, 109–11

Lamott, Anne, 8
late papers, 8
LeCren, Carole, 98
Lee, Harper, 16–19
letters
    to next year's students, 81
    to parents, about reading drafts, 105
    as persuasive writing, 33
    recommending titles for curriculum, 81
    to teachers, about revision, 111, 115–16
Lincoln, Abraham, 84
literature
    comparing films to, 88–94
    generating questions about, 9–10
    as movies, 81
literature responses, 61–81
    authentic, 9–10, 81
    California Standards Test Scoring Rubric, 62–66
    question papers, 9–13
    rubrics for, 66–74
Louria, Meredith, 77
low-stakes writing, 85–86

"Maintenance" (Nye), 24
"Man in the Water, The" (Rosenblatt), 27–28
mechanical errors, 5–6, 97–98
memories, triggering with smells, 51–52
metacognitive dialogues, for question papers, 12–13
Miller, Arthur, 79
misplaced modifiers, 97
model essays, 23–25
model question papers, 10–11
Moffett, James, 98–99
"Mother Tongue" (Tan), 25

movies
  comparing literature to, 88–94
  literature as, 81
  R-rated, 88
multiple traits scoring, 66–67
My Ántonia (Cather), 20–21

narrative writing, 39–59. *See also* cohesive writing;
      writing
  autobiographical, 62–66
  California Standards Test Scoring Rubric, 62–66
  constructive criticism on, 39
  creating characters, 51
  creating setting, 51–52
  fictional, 62–66
  interest in, 48–49
  prompts for, 50
  reflections on, 48, 111, 115–16
  standards for, 49–50
  teacher concerns about, 48–49
  writing exercises for, 50–59
National Assessment of Educational Progress
      (NAEP), 1
  eighth-grade persuasive writing prompt, 35–37
  twelfth-grade persuasive writing prompt, 37–38
  Writing Assessment, 2
  Writing Report Card, 38
  writing test, 15
National Council of Teachers of English (NCTE),
      105
National Writing Project, 15
newspapers
  editorials, 31
  ideas for essay topics from, 31
  news stories *vs.* editorials, 32
news stories
  editorials *vs.*, 32
  selecting from newspaper, 31
  writing opinion pieces on, 32–33
non-English-speaking families, 103
Northwest Regional Laboratories, 66
Norton Book of Personal Essays, 23
nouns, 96–97
"No Wonder They Call Me a Bitch" (Hodgman), 25
Nye, Naomi Shihab, 24

Olathe Unified School District, Kansas, 66
One Flew over the Cuckoo's Nest (Kesey), 88
One Flew over the Cuckoo's Nest (movie), 88
On Writing (King), 96
opening sentences, 104, 106
opinion pieces, writing about news stories, 32–33
ordering events, 52–53
Other People's Children (Delpit), 117–18
Outbreak, 88, 92–94

parallelism, 97
parents
  feedback from, 103–4
  letters to, 105
Payne, Michele, 49
peer editing, 98–99, 102–4
Peer Response Sheet, 102
Pelton, Claire, 9
perfectionism, 8
personal essays, models of, 23
personalized prompts, 20–21
personal qualities, writing about, 54–55
persuasive writing, 30–38
  about news stories, 32–33
  California Standards Test Scoring Rubric, 62–
      66
  defined, 32
  general characteristics of, 33–34
  informational writing *vs.*, 32
  letters as, 33
Plath, Sylvia, 14–15
poetry, 80
point method, 89–90
point of view, 52
Portfolio Checklist (form), 112
portfolios
  reflections and, 111
  self-assessment of, 111, 114
  student performance and, 74
Portfolio Self-Assessment (form), 114
prepositional phrases, 106
Preston, Richard, 88, 92–94
  prompts, 14–21
  authentic, 36–37, 118
  College Board, 20
  directions in, 18
  importance of, 15–16
  NAEP eighth-grade, 35–37
  NAEP twelfth-grade, 37–38
  for narrative writing, 50
  personalized, 20–21
  for persuasive writing, 35–38
  problems with, 118
  questions to ask about, 20
  revising, 17–20
  thesis statements in response to, 17

qualifiers, 96
question papers, 9–13
  metacognitive dialogues, 12–13
  model, for "She Walks in Beauty," 10–11
  moving to drafting from, 13–14
  question and sentence openers for, 11
  small groups for, 11–12
  value of, 11

quickwrites
    expository essays *vs.*, 13
        assessment of, 86–87
        saving, 87
        teacher response to, 87
        types of, 86–87
quotations
    analyzing words or images from, 77–78
    effective use of, 77–80
    Reflections charts for, 74–77

reading
    essays, 23, 24–25
    like a writer, 25–26
    student writing, 23–24
Reading Log (form), 113
reading logs, 111
reflections
    on narrative writing, 48, 111, 115–16
    portfolios and, 111
Reflections charts, 74–77
refutation, of opposing arguments, 36
responses to literature. *See* literature responses
revision
    authentic, 104–6
    cohesive writing and, 119
    evaluating, 108
    in five-day writing plan, 89
    letters to teachers about, 111, 115–16
Rich, Adrienne, 12
Rodriquez, Richard, 67, 69–72
Rogers, Joe, 3
Rosenblatt, Roger, 27–28
R-rated films, 88
rubrics
    classroom, 62
    custom-written, 66
    four-point scale, 62, 63–66
    for literature responses, 66–74
    for scoring standardized tests, 62
    six-point scale, 62, 68, 107
    unclassifiable writing and, 69
run-together sentences, 97

Santa Monica High School, 5, 62
scaffolding, 74–77
self-assessment, 106–16
    culminating assignment, 111
    of portfolios, 111, 114
sentences
    ending in prepositional phrases, 106
    fragments, 97
    openers for question papers, 11
    opening, 104–5
    revising, 106
    run-together, 97

"There are/There is," 98
    variety in, 104
settings, writing exercise, 51–52
"She Walks in Beauty" (Byron), 10–11
"Signs, The" (Bennett), 39–48
"Silent Dancing" (Cofer), 25
six-point rubrics, 62, 68, 107
small groups
    for five-day writing plan, 90–91
    reading essays in, 26
    writing question papers in, 11–12
smell, triggering memories with, 51–52
spelling, 99
Stafford, William, 50–51
standardized tests
    narrative writing, 49–50
    rubrics for scoring, 62
    writing proficiency criteria, 2–3
    writing samples in, 1–2
Steven, Wallace, 80
Storms, Barbara, 15–16
struggling writers, 73–77
    confidence of, 74
    problems of, 73
    scaffolding for, 74–77
Student papers
    "Blue Paradise" (McDaniel), 69–70
    "Emotional Isolation" (Eggebroten), 71–71
    "Let Books Be Books" (Sernas), 92–94
    "Signs, The" (Bennett), 39–48
    "Simple Minds" (Phelps), 109–11
Students
    Argueta, Nancy, 79
    Bennett, Claire, 39–48
    Cook, Heather, 98
    Eggebroten, Ellen, 71–71, 74
    Egziabher, Michael, 115
    Escalera, Alicia, 14–15, 20–21
    Greenberg, Rachel, 115
    Kamins, Marni, 13–14
    Len, Jackie, 78
    McDaniel, Eva, 69–70
    Montoya, Paloma, 73–74
    Oyenoki, Aimee, 115
    Phelps, Emily, 107, 109–11
    Ryan, Katie, 79
    Sernas, Arturo, 92–94
    Sherman, Aaron, 78
    Vasquez, Yvette, 79
student writing
    about abuse, 48–49
    lack of cohesiveness in, 7
    posting, 24
    reading out loud, 24
    rubrics and, 69
    student reading of, 23–24

summary writing, California Standards Test Scoring Rubric, 62–66

Tan, Amy, 13–14, 25
teachers, as coaches, 97
teacher/student dialog journals, 87
Teaching the Universe of Discourse (Moffett), 98–99
textbooks, 23–24, 24
"There are/There is" sentences, 98
thesis statements
  developing, 90
  discovering, 84
  evidence for, 25, 30
  finding, in an essay, 25, 30
  in response to prompts, 17
thinking, through writing, 6, 83–85, 87
"Thirteen Ways of Looking at a Blackbird" (Stevens), 80
"This is a Photograph of Me" (Atwood), 12
thousand-word essays, 8–9
timed-writing assignments, 91
time line, for college essays, 54–55
To Kill a Mockingbird (Lee), 16–19
topics
  for essays, 27–28
  from newspapers, 31
  ordinary, writing in style of author, 80
  selecting, 30–31
"To Sleep Under the Stars" (Graham), 61–62
"trauma" stories, 48–49

Uncensored Conference on Youth Education (Colorado), 3–4

verbs, 96, 97
violent behavior, teacher reporting of, 48–49

"Way of Writing, A" (Strafford), 50–51
Weiss, Philip, 24
White, E. B., 96
Williams, William Carlos, 115
Wolff, Tobias, 61, 81
Woman Warrior, The (Kingston), 74, 75–77
Wright, Frank Lloyd, 7
writers, reading like, 25–26
Writers Need Readers (form), 104
writing. *See also* cohesive writing; narrative writing; persuasive writing
  about abuse, 48–49
  analytic, 67, 68
  before class discussion, 30
  expository, 31–32
  free-form, 9
  freewriting, 13

getting started, 8–9, 9
inertia in, 9
informational, 31–32
learning about self through, 6, 83–85, 87
proficiency criteria, 2–3
prompts for, 14–21
quality of writing assignment and, 15–16
student practice in, 85–87
thinking through, 6, 83–85, 87
value of, 2
volume of, 83–84, 85–87
writing assignments. *See also* writing exercises
  comparison/contrast, 88–94
  culminating, 80–81
  high-stakes, 88
  in-class, 85–86
  late, 8
  low-stakes, 85–86
  timed, 91
  writing quality and, 15–16
writing conferences, on drafts, 33–34
writing exercises. *See also* writing assignments
  autobiographical narration, 53–59
  characters, 51, 52
  college essays, 53–59
  dialogue, 53
  inertia, 9
  for narrative writing, 50–59
  ordering events, 52–53
  point of view, 52
  settings, 51–52
writing instruction
  analysis of, 15–16
  in analytic writing, 67
  beliefs about, 85, 118
  five-day writing plan, 88–94
  guidelines for, 85, 118
  lack of cohesiveness in, 7
  narrative writing, 50–59
  portfolios and, 74
  student-defined problems and solutions, 3–5
  writing to learn, 85–87
writing process, 83–85
  features of, 1
  student approach to, 83
writing prompts. *See* prompts
Writing Report Card (NAEP), 38
writing samples, in standardized tests, 1–2
writing style, of authors, 80
"writing-to-learn" papers, 85–87
  about homework, 87
  quickwrites, 85–87

"Yes Ma'am, No, Sir" (Yago), 28–30

Beyond Standards
Excellence in the High School English Classroom
Foreword by **Sheridan Blau**

"It's a crime," Carol Jago declares, "to let any students—whatever their native abilities—drift through the school year without effort, without growth, without goals. Each student is capable of achieving excellence. But it requires a nurturing, vigorous classroom environment— not the glass ceilings set by even the best of standards-based instruction."

To help current and future high school English teachers create and maintain this kind of environment, Jago has created this groundbreaking book. *Beyond Standards* offers concrete ways to reconceive what it means to foster excellent performance in the classroom and vivid examples of student work that was motivated by the pursuit of excellence rather than by test scores. Packed with richly detailed classroom anecdotes, it explores the many ways teachers can select books, design lessons, and inspire discussions that can lead all their students to extraordinary achievements, both in the study of literature and in their writing assignments. Included are practical tips on everything from helping students self-edit their writing to "tricking" them into reading a lot more poetry.

Beyond Standards may be seen as a series of stories—or "ethnographic studies"—on how to make the work of the high school English class humanly and genuinely important to students so that they will engage in literate activity with the same kind of attention and effort as "real" writers. Under such conditions, Jago asserts, students will learn more and produce more useful and impressive products than any standards document could possibly anticipate.

0-86709-503-2 / 2001 / 106pp / Paper / $15.00

Prices subject to change.

Heinemann
www.heinemann.com